2 Corinthi
and Pa

2 Corinthians: A Short Exegetical and Pastoral Commentary

Anthony C. Thiselton

CASCADE *Books* • Eugene, Oregon

2 CORINTHIANS: A SHORT EXEGETICAL AND PASTORAL COMMENTARY

Copyright © 2019 Anthony C. Thiselton. All rights reserved. Except for brief quotations in critical publications or reviews, no part of this book may be reproduced in any manner without prior written permission from the publisher. Write: Permissions, Wipf and Stock Publishers, 199 W. 8th Ave., Suite 3, Eugene, OR 97401.

Cascade Books
An Imprint of Wipf and Stock Publishers
199 W. 8th Ave., Suite 3
Eugene, OR 97401

www.wipfandstock.com

PAPERBACK ISBN: 978-1-5326-7270-5
HARDCOVER ISBN: 978-1-5326-7271-2
EBOOK ISBN: 978-1-5326-7272-9

Cataloguing-in-Publication data:

Names: Thiselton, Anthony C., author.

Title: 2 Corinthians: a short exegetical and pastoral commentary / by Anthony C. Thiselton.

Description: Eugene, OR: Cascade Books, 2019 | Includes bibliographical references and index.

Identifiers: ISBN 978-1-5326-7270-5 (paperback) | ISBN 978-1-5326-7271-2 (hardcover) | ISBN 978-1-5326-7272-9 (ebook)

Subjects: LCSH: Bible—Corinthians, 2nd—Commentaries.

Classification: LCC BS2675.3 T44 2019 (print) | LCC BS2675.3 (ebook)

Unless indicated otherwise, Scripture quotations are from the New Revised Standard Version Bible, copyright © 1989 National Council of the Churches of Christ in the United States of America. Used by permission. All rights reserved.

Manufactured in the U.S.A.   09/12/19

Rosemary, for her ceaseless support over fifty-six years of marriage, and Rev. Stuart Dyas for his very sage advice and meticulous corrections of typos, grammar, and style.

CONTENTS

Preface | xi

Part I: Introduction

A. Paul and Corinth | 3
B. Roman Corinth | 4
   1. *A prosperous, bustling, international community* 4
   2. *Corinth as a Roman colony* 5
   3. *Corinth as a hub of manufacturing, patronage, and business* 6
   4. *The ethos of the city permeated the church and resonates with today* 7
C. The Content and Argument of the Epistle | 8
   1. *Broad outline* 8
   2. *The unity of 2 Corinthians* 9
D. Fundamental Framing Questions | 12
   1. *The identity of Paul's opponents* 12
   2. *The tearful letter* 13
   3. *Doctrinal themes* 13
   4. *Paul: apostle, missionary pastor, and man of intense emotions* 15

Part II: Exegesis

I. Introduction (1:1–11) | 19

   1. Address (1:1-2)   19

   2. Thanksgiving and hope (1:3-11)   21

II. Defense of Paul's Conduct with Regard to His Travel Plans and the Offender (1:12—2:17) | 28

   1. The theme of boasting or glorying (1:12-14)   28

   2. The postponement of Paul's intended visit (1:15-22)   30

   3. Whether or not Paul's plans change, his purpose remains (1:23—2:4)   33

   4. The need to forgive the one who has caused such pain (2:5-11)   35

   5. A further reason why Paul changed his travel plans (2:12-13)   37

   6. The glory of ministry and God's triumphal procession (2:14-17)   38

III. The Authentic Ministry Described and Defended (3:1—7:4) | 42

   1. Paul's ministry to the Corinthians (3:1-6)   42

   2. The ministry of the Spirit: Paul's reflection on Exodus 34:29-35 (3:7-18)   47

   3. A ministry of integrity (4:1-6)   51

   4. The treasure of the gospel through fragile earthenware jars (4:7-15)   56

   5. The present and the future as seen and unseen: longing to be clothed (4:16—5:10)   61

   6. The ministry of reconciliation (5:11—6:2)   70

   7. The apostolic credentials of Paul's mission (6:3-10)   77

   8. A plea for openness and purity: the temple of the Living God (6:11—7:4)   81

CONTENTS

IV. The Arrival of Titus in Macedonia (7:5–16) | 87

    1. The encouraging report brought by Titus after a difficult situation (7:5–7)   87

    2. The long-term positive effects of Paul's letter (7:8–13a)   89

    3. The joy of Titus at the Corinthians' response (7:13b–16)   91

V. The Collection for Poor Christians in Jerusalem (8:1—9:15) | 93

    1. Paul's exhortation to finish the collection (8:1–15)   93

    2. Titus' eagerness to travel to Corinth again (8:16—9:5)   99

    3. Wider reflections on giving and the generosity of God (9:6–15)   103

VI. Paul Confronts the Malignant Ministry of His Opponents (10:1—13:13) | 108

    1. Present or absent, Paul's authority is the same (10:1–11)   109

    2. Paul and his rivals: proper and improper boasting (10:12–18)   115

    3. Paul's use of "the speech of the fool": to which Christ did he pledge the Corinthians? (11:1–4)   118

    4. The "foolish" speech continues: Paul and the "super-apostles" (11:5–15)   121

    5. Paul boasts about his sufferings (11:16–33)   124

    6. Paul's visions and revelation, the climax of "the fool's speech" (12:1–13)   128

    7. Preparation for Paul's third visit to Corinth and final greeting (12:14—13:4)   133

    8. An authentication of faith, the purpose of Paul's letter, and final greetings and benediction (13:5–13)   137

Bibliography | 141

Index of Names | 147

Index of Subjects | 149

Index of Biblical References | 155

PREFACE

The title *2 Corinthians: A Short Exegetical and Pastoral Commentary* was chosen to constitute an explicit parallel to my earlier book, *1 Corinthians: A Shorter Exegetical and Pastoral Commentary* (Eerdmans, 2006). This shorter commentary followed my *The First Epistle to the Corinthians: A Commentary on the Greek Text* (Eerdmans, 2000, NIGTC). In the case of 2 Corinthians, I have decided not to produce a larger commentary on the Greek text, largely because, as I shall explain, an abundance of good larger and more detailed commentaries is now available.

Having spent a number of years on 1 Corinthians it has always been my hope to complete Paul's correspondence with the church in Corinth by writing on 2 Corinthians. As Barnett remarks, Paul's relationships with the Corinthians span a seven-year period. In A.D. 50-52, he spent a year and half in Corinth establishing the church. Sometime in 55 or 56 he made a second visit (2 Cor 13:2), what he calls a "painful visit," to deal with an emergency disciplinary problem in the church. In 56 or 57, he came to Corinth for the third time (13:1) and stayed for three months before taking his leave of them. Paul's relations with Corinth may not have been his happiest, but they were probably more intense and prolonged than with any other Christian community. 2 Corinthians is full of heartfelt emotion. But it is also full of confidence in Christ and the resurrection, and personal reflections on apostolicity and the ministry. It shows how power and authority are seen through human weakness and humility. The subtitle of Barnett's shorter study, "Power in Weakness," hits the nail on the head.

So in addition to its intense emotion, 2 Corinthians is no less "theological" or "doctrinal" than Romans and 1 Corinthians. In my commentary on 1 Corinthians, I lamented that Paul's emphasis on free grace in 1 Corinthians had too often been overshadowed by attention to this theme in Romans. Much the same may be said of crucial themes in 2 Corinthians. So just as I produced *A Shorter Exegetical and Pastoral Commentary* on 1 Corinthians, so now I offer a short commentary on 2 Corinthians for those who do not wish to comb through several hundred pages of more detailed studies. This stands alongside my two commentaries on 1 Corinthians, my medium-length commentary on Romans (SPCK and Eerdmans, 2016), and my reception-history of 1 and 2 Thessalonians (*1 and 2 Thessalonians through the Centuries*, Wiley-Blackwell, 2011).

Meanwhile, I must explain why I judge that there is already more than an adequacy of detailed longer commentaries on 2 Corinthians, which releases me to write a short commentary on this letter. Margaret Thrall's very detailed two-volume New International Critical Commentary (T. & T. Clark, 1994 & 2000, 977 pages) superseded the excellent I.C.C. commentary by Alfred Plummer (1915). She was Reader in Biblical Studies at Bangor and a meticulous expert in New Testament Greek. Although they are also deeply pastoral, the two commentaries by George H. Guthrie (Baker Academic, 2015, 710 pages) and by Paul Barnett (New International Commentary, Eerdmans, 1997, 662 pages) are of outstanding value and insight. My small work owes much to them. Mention must also be made of four other detailed commentaries: Ralph P. Martin (Word Biblical Commentary, 1991, 529 pages), Murray J. Harris (NIGTC, Eerdmans, 2015, 989 pages), Victor P. Furnish (Anchor Bible, Doubleday, 1984, 619 pages), and Philip E. Hughes (Marshall, 1961, 508 pages). All these shed a flood of light on current New Testament scholarship and exegetical issues. In the light of these seven major commentaries, it would have been unnecessary or even presumptuous to attempt yet another longer, detailed commentary along the lines of my work on 1 Corinthians, which at the time (2000) constituted a unique pioneer project among English commentaries.

A further distinguishing feature of this short commentary is the series of "questions for reflection," which are designed to ask practical questions for Christians in today's world. It is these questions that are signified by the word "pastoral" in the title.

PREFACE

In addition to my debt to the seven commentaries cited above, together with numerous specialist studies on Paul's theology, I am indebted to support from my wife Rosemary, who also assisted with indexing, and to the Revd. Stuart Dyas for his meticulous proof-reading and advice.

Anthony C. Thiselton, D.D., FKC, FBA,

Emeritus Professor of Christian Theology, Universities of Nottingham and Chester, and Emeritus Canon Theologian of Leicester and of Southwell & Nottingham

PART I
INTRODUCTION

INTRODUCTION

A. Paul and Corinth

Paul had written 1 Corinthians in the early months of AD 54. But it was only partially successful. Some concerns were probably dealt with: for instance, we hear no more disputation about the resurrection of the body, or the eating of food sacrificed to idols, and references to gnosis and wisdom become much less common. The cause of the new troubles entered Corinth *from without.*

As Paul Barnett notes, the Corinthian church proved to be the most demanding of the churches Paul had oversight of. In 1 Corinthians Paul writes objectively and confidently, while 2 Corinthians reveals a range of emotional extremes. But in both letters he is forced to defend his doctrines.[1]

It is unfortunate that because Romans is more systematic and often easier to follow, historically it has put the Corinthian epistles in the shade, although justification by sovereign grace is not absent, and is thoroughly applied. "What do you have that you did not receive?" Paul asked the church in Corinth; "and if you received it, why do you boast as if it were not a gift?" (1 Cor 4:7). And in their way, the Corinthians epistles are no less theologically rich and deserving of attention.

---

1. Barnett, *The Message of 2 Corinthians*, 13–14.

PART I: INTRODUCTION

B. Roman Corinth

No introduction to 2 Corinthians, however short, would be adequate without a careful explanation of the distinctive features of the city of Corinth.[2]

1. A Prosperous, bustling, international community

Corinth was one of the most vibrant, exciting, and challenging cities in the whole of the Greek world in Roman times. It was situated on a narrow neck of land in Greece with a harbor on each side of it. On the east side, the harbor of Cenchreae faces across the sea to the Roman province of Asia and Ephesus. On the west side the port of Lechaeum faces Italy and ultimately Rome. Yet at the narrowest point of the isthmus the distance between the two seacoasts is less than six miles, or barely nine km. Corinth was thus a major center for international east-west trade.

This favored location for east-west trade was matched by an almost equally favored position between northern and southern Greece. To the north lay the Province of Achaea, and yet further north, Macedonia, which included Philippi and Thessalonica. To the south lay the Peloponnese, down to the shores of Cape Malea. Corinth stood at the crossroads or intersection between north and south and between east and west for business and trade. In Paul's time it had become a busy, bustling, cosmopolitan business center. By comparison, Athens might have seemed a slumbering university city, dreaming simply of its greater past.

Those who traded between Asia and the west preferred to use the two port facilities of Corinth rather than travel by ship around Cape Malia, where winds and tides were often hazardous off the southern shores of Greece, especially in winter. If they used light cargo ships, sailors or traders could transport even the ship on rollers over the paved road, called the *diolkos*, that linked the two harbours. Alternatively, they could unload cargo at one port and reload it at the other. In either case, toll fees or carriage charges swelled the income of Corinth and its officials.

Corinth inherited a large income from tourism, business, and manufacturing. Tourists flocked to Corinth, not least for the famous Isthmian

---

2. I shall repeat many of the features that I noted in my earlier commentaries on 1 Corinthians (2000 and 2006). In this particular section, I am going to draw especially on what I have written in my shorter commentary on 1 Corinthians of 2006, together with a few comments from Donald Engels, *Roman Corinth* (1990). I have not seen clearer or more relevant material elsewhere.

Games, which were held every two years. Second only to the Olympic Games, the Isthmian games were among the three great games-festivals of the whole of Greece. They attracted participants, spectators, and other visitors from all corners of the Empire between Rome and the east. Archaeologists have recovered coins that witness to the range of international visitors who came to the Games.

When he first arrived in Corinth, Paul would probably have seen whatever booths and stands remained from the Games of AD 49, and they would have been in full swing during his ministry there in AD 51. By the middle of the first century, the Games had expanded to include a multiplicity of competitive and sometimes spectacular events. In addition to chariot races, athletic events, competitions in trumpet, flute, and lyre, poetry readings, and other events, Corinth or Isthmia had, unusually, introduced athletic contests for women, and the *apobatikon*, in which a rider would leap from one team of horses to another. During this period Corinth managed the Games and reaped a vast income from them.

In addition to competitors and spectators, business people, traders, and especially individuals with entrepreneurial skills or hopes visited what constituted a hub of opportunity for new commercial contacts and ventures, new possibilities of employment, quick person-to-person agreements or transactions, and a large cosmopolitan pool of potential consumers. These visitors brought money to rent rooms, to buy necessary or exotic products, and to hire dockers, porters, secretaries, accountants, guides, bodyguards, blacksmiths, carpenters, cooks, housekeepers, and both literate and menial slaves. They sought to employ or to hire managers, craftsmen, and people who could repair wagons, tents, ships, or chariots. This list conveys a good idea of the composition of the average Pauline church community.

Paul would have spent many long, hot hours in a workshop, probably close to the Lechaeum Road or on the north, sun-drenched side of the Forum or *Agora*. Archaeologists have excavated shops or workshops of some 13' x 8', some with sleeping accommodation above, which Aquila and Priscilla may well have used as their quarters (Acts 18:3).

2. Corinth as a Roman colony

Corinth was a Roman colony that welcomed waves of new settlers. Corinth's geographical position as an international centre of trade, together with its attraction for business and economic prosperity, already sets the stage for regarding it as a deeply competitive, self-sufficient, and entrepreneurial culture, marked by ambitions to succeed at what we nowadays term a corporate mind shaped by consumerism, and perhaps even with its own celebrities.

Two further factors add decisively to this developing picture. The history of Corinth goes far back into earlier centuries as a Greek city-state, but in the second century BC it became embroiled in political struggles that related to Sparta and also to Rome. In 146 BC, a Roman army sacked the city and left it virtually in ruins for some two hundred years. Yet such a prime location for defence, trade, and economic power could not remain neglected forever. In 44 BC, the year of his assassination, Julius Caesar re-founded Corinth as a Roman *colonia* for veterans from his legions.

The new Corinth was initially resettled chiefly by Roman soldiers, Roman freedpersons, and Roman slaves, and was very soon swelled by tradespersons and business entrepreneurs from various parts of the Roman Republic. The government and laws of the new city were established on a fully Roman pattern. Loyalty to Rome was fundamental to the settlement of the veterans, and loyal Roman citizens made Corinth a secure strategic base for possible future campaigns against Parthia, Dacia, or further east. The new name of the city honored Julius Caesar: *Colonia Laus Julia Corinthiensis* in full, or Corinth for short. The towering mountainous hill AcroCorinth, some 570 meters from the city center, had served as a citadel for defense during the early Greek period, and it still provided a structure for defense if ever this was needed.

The well-ordered colony attracted an increasing number of immigrants, who came in the hope of making their fortune. Every condition was right: a cosmopolitan international center under secure Roman government order, with shipping routes to Rome and Ephesus and to the east; a plentiful supply of natural resources for manufacturing; and a vibrant business mentality where quick success (or sometimes failure) was part of the cultural ethos. Competition, patronage, consumerism, and multiform layers and levels of success were part of the air breathed by citizens of Corinth.

3. Corinth as a hub of manufacturing, patronage, and business

As if all this were not enough, Corinth enjoyed spectacular natural resources for the production of goods. First and foremost, the almost limitless supply of water from the Pyrenean Fountains not only provided the domestic needs of a large, vibrant, expanding city, but was also a necessary component for the manufacture of bricks, pottery, roof tiles, terracotta ornaments, and utensils. Other needed components were available: a very large deposit of marl and clay; light sandstone to be quarried or used for building on a large scale; and a harder limestone for durable paving on streets and roads.

Even in the earlier Greek period, Corinth had been called "wealthy Corinth." In its first-century Roman period, the city hummed with economic wealth, business, and expansion. Businesswomen like Chloe, we may surmise, sent their middle managers to Corinth to deal on their behalf (1:10). Aquila and Priscilla saw Corinth as a prime location for leather goods or tentmaking when Claudius expelled Jews from Rome in AD 49. They probably arrived, already as Christians, shortly before Paul, and set up their workroom-come-shop either on the north side of the Forum or among the shops and markets of the Lechaeum Road.

It is not surprising that the culture of the day in Corinth expressed a degree of *self-satisfaction*, if not *complacency*, alongside the *drive to compete and to succeed*. The culture was one of *self-promotion*. When Paul carried the gospel to Corinth, it is not surprising that he "came . . . with much fear and trembling" (2:3). The gospel of a humiliated, crucified Christ was an *affront* to the people who cherished *success* and loved *winning*. Paul refused to carry himself like a professional lecturer or rhetorician, which in 2 Corinthians meant his insistence on preaching the gospel free of charge. And, as he says in 1 Cor 2:2, the gospel he preached among them declared nothing "except Jesus Christ, and him crucified."

4. The ethos of the city permeated the church and resonates with today

Study of both 1 and 2 Corinthians makes it clear that Christians in Corinth still carried over into their Christian existence many of the cultural traits that characterized their pre-Christian culture. Christians are always *in process* of renewal and sanctification, betraying signs of the old life as well as signs of the new. One writer has compared this to coming out of the cold into a warm room: pockets of ice from the cold may remain, even when we have decisively come under the influence of heat and warmth. The heat is decisive, but traces of the cold remain in the present. In the case of the Corinthians, some competitiveness, self-achievement, self-promotion, self-congratulation, and self-sufficiency remained, even if these were no longer decisive for their Christian lives.

PART I: INTRODUCTION

Competition and success were everywhere apparent: in the Isthmian games, in business and trade, in social status, and in economic power. Entrepreneurs regularly used social networks of influence, and this occurred not least in Corinth through the Roman system of patronage, where choosing the right patron could secure rapid promotion through the influences of the patron rather than through personal merit. Paul's opponents in 2 Corinthians readily showed how they could "put down" others and boast or brag about their own achievements. The so-called false apostles looked for a triumphalist gospel rather than a crucified Christ. We must beware of similar attendances in the culture of our own day, whereby consumerism, celebrity cults, and self-promotion, often threaten to crowd out the relevance of the crucified and risen Christ.

C. The Content and Argument of the Epistle

1. Broad outline

2 Corinthians has three clearly-marked divisions. Chapters 1–7 consist mainly of an exposition of Paul's apostolic ministry. Chapters 8–9 plead the cause of a collection organized among the gentile churches for the church of Jerusalem. Chapters 10–13 strongly defend Paul's apostolic authority in the face of its denial by people in Corinth. Nevertheless, it is crucial to regard these sections not as independent themes, but as part of an integrated whole, as David R. Hall and, earlier, George Beasley-Murray, among many others, rightly stress.[3]

2 Corinthians is also perhaps the most neglected of Paul's major letters (often studied less than his popular shorter letters), but this is surprising because "this letter is the most moving document that Paul has left to us."[4] In the light of this neglect, there is a need for a relatively short introduction to this epistle. Other introductions often seem to some to be unduly complex because, as C. K. Barrett notes, there is a serious danger of arguing in a circle, i.e., from historical reconstruction to literary hypothesis, and from literary hypothesis back to historical reconstruction.[5]

---

3. Hall, *The Unity of the Corinthian Correspondence*; Beasley-Murray, "Introduction," 1–3.
4. Beasley-Murray, "Introduction," 6.
5. Barrett, *The Second Epistle to the Corinthians*.

INTRODUCTION

2. The unity of 2 Corinthians

It is understandable that for several centuries scholars have proposed that 2 Corinthians 1–9 is not the same letter as 2 Corinthians 10–13. Whereas in chapters 1–7 (or 1–9), Paul expresses his joy because he and the congregation have made up their quarrel and he can even warn about too strict a punishment of the unrighteous (2:7-8), 10:1 begins anew with "I, Paul, myself"; he attacks "some" (10:2), "such people" (10:11), "those who would like to claim" (11:12), "false apostles" (11:13), servants of Satan, "who disguise themselves as servants of righteousness" (11:15), etc.[6] This basic partition theory—that our letter of 2 Corinthians is composed of two originally separate letters that have been joined—has been held since at least 1776, when it was proposed by J. S. Semler. More recently it has been held by Windisch, Héring, T. W. Manson, and many others. Yet it has generated fierce debate. And whatever our views on partition theses, most writers regard the whole of 2 Corinthians as written by Paul, even if on separate occasions. Thrall writes, "It is certain that it is genuinely Pauline."[7]

There are other less simple partition theories. Thrall and others regard chapters 8 and 9, on the collection for Jerusalem, to be too repetitive plausibly to have been written on the very same occasion.[8] Some also question whether 2:14—7:1 was written at the same time as the rest of 2 Corinthians. But against partition theories, a growing number of moderate scholars support the unity of 2 Corinthians. These include C. K. Barrett, Frances Young and David Ford, Paul Barnett, George H. Guthrie, and most decisively David R. Hall in his book *The Unity of the Corinthian Correspondence*.[9] One important factor is that Hall pays attention to 1 Corinthians, which is one of my main reasons for passionately supporting arguments for the unity of the epistle.

Hall rightly argues that what he calls "puffed-upness" at Corinth dominates 1 and 2 Corinthians equally. He writes, "Being blown up with self-importance like the frog in Aesop's Fables . . . occurs three times in (1 Corinthians) chapter 4, and three times in chapters 5–16."[10] Further ex-

---

6. Kümmel, *Introduction to the New Testament*, 211–12.
7. Thrall, *The Second Epistle to the Corinthians*, 3.
8. Thrall, *The Second Epistle to the Corinthians*, 4.
9. Barrett, *The Second Epistle to the Corinthians*, 6–36; Young and Ford, *Meaning and Truth in 2 Corinthians*, 36–44; Barnett, *The Second Epistle to the Corinthians*; Guthrie, *2 Corinthians*, 23–38; Hall, *The Unity of the Corinthian Correspondence*.
10. Hall, *The Unity of the Corinthian Correspondence*, 32.

amination, he says, reveals the continuity between the competitive pursuit of "wisdom" rebuked in chapters 1–4, and the behavioral problems discussed in chapters 5–16. "There is a continuity between the puffed-upness of [some] Greek *tines*, who were defying Paul's authority in 4:18–19 and the puffed-upness of the church as a whole in 5:5."[11] 6:13 implies a separation between the physical and the spiritual, as in 1 Cor 5:1–5.[12] Hall further comments on chapters 8–10, on the eating of meals. He adds a chapter on the social background of 1 Corinthians, rightly referring to Gerd Theissen, Jerome Murphy O'Connor, Dale Martin, and others.[13]

On 2 Corinthians, Hall does not deny the huge psychological difference between 2 Corinthians 1–9 and chapters 10–13.[14] He quotes Plummer as saying, Paul "suddenly bursts out into a torrent of reproaches, sarcastic self-vindication, and stern warnings, which must almost have undermined the pacific effect of the first seven chapters."[15] He also quotes Jerome Murphy-O'Connor to the same effect.[16] His reply to the partitionists, however, makes several points. First, "Paul's criticisms are mainly directed at the incoming teachers, not at the church."[17] In addition to the text itself, he also quotes Barrett and Hughes in support. Hughes points out that 10:1 begins not with an outburst but with entreaty "by the meekness and gentleness of Christ."[18] He writes as their father, not as judge. Second, rhetoric in the ancient Greco-Roman world often allowed or encouraged confrontational approaches. Danker illustrates this from the speeches of Demosthenes.[19] Young and Ford support this argument, and Hughes also cites parallels from Cicero. Third, Hall argues that the historical situation demands different responses in chapters 10–13 from 1–9. The final three chapters, he observes, concern a personal confrontation with rivals.[20]

---

11. Hall, *The Unity of the Corinthian Correspondence*, 34.
12. Hall, *The Unity of the Corinthian Correspondence*, 37.
13. Hall, *The Unity of the Corinthian Correspondence*, 51–85.
14. Hall, *The Unity of the Corinthian Correspondence*, 87–89.
15. Plummer, *A Critical and Exegetical Commentary*, xx1x–xxx; Hall, *The Unity of the Corinthian Correspondence*, 88.
16. Murphy O'Connor, *The Theology of the Second Letter to the Corinthians*, 10–11.
17. Hall, *The Unity of the Corinthian Correspondence*, 88.
18. Hughes, *Paul's Second Epistle to the Corinthians*, xxiii.
19. Danker, "Paul's Debt to the *De Corona* of Demosthenes."
20. Hall, *The Unity of the Corinthian Correspondence*, 88 and 92–100.

INTRODUCTION

Hall also considers arguments about chapters 8 and 9. He writes, "A further objection to the unity of two Corinthians is the central place of the appeal for the collection. In opposing the view of Young and Ford, 2 Corinthians has a style of a forensic defence. Murphy-O'Connor protests that 'a plea for money, even for others, has no place in an apologia.'" He continues, "But this does not invalidate the view that Paul regarded the letter in broad terms as an apology, but with various other items thrown in."[21] Hall points out issues relating to Titus as an example. He also quotes R. F. Collins as suggesting that it is not legitimate to expect perfect unity in any letter.[22] He concludes, "The general tone of chapters 8 and 9 is in keeping with 2 Corinthians as a whole."[23] He returns to consider these arguments further in a later chapter, engaging the work of Hans Dieter Betz.[24] Hall approves of Ben Witherington's argument that the Corinthian correspondence represents a "mixed" list of topics.[25]

Finally, Hall addresses the question of vocabulary. The change from plural to singular (e.g., "I myself, Paul" in 10:1) is no argument for the partition of the epistle, especially since this change of number is precisely what we should expect when Paul addresses his personal rivals.[26] As far as examples of non-Pauline vocabulary are concerned, Paul could well be borrowing the language of his opponents.[27] He concludes, "None of the arguments commonly used for separating chapters 10–13 from the rest of 2 Corinthians stands up to examination. We should therefore accept the testimony of the manuscripts of the early church that the letter is a unity."[28] Hall's arguments are strong, but in the light of other arguments by C. K. Barrett, Young and Ford, George Guthrie, Paul Barnett, and others, they become entirely convincing. They are especially so in the light of his careful exposition of 1 Corinthians. Thus, in the following commentary, I shall be reading 2 Corinthians as a single, coherent letter.

---

21. Hall, *The Unity of the Corinthian Correspondence*, 100; cf. Murphy-O'Connor, *Theology*, 11.
22. R. F. Collins, "Reflections on one Corinthians as a Hellenistic letter," 60.
23. Hall, *The Unity of the Corinthian Correspondence*, 101.
24. Hall, *The Unity of the Corinthian Correspondence*, 114–19.
25. Witherington, *Conflict and Community in Corinth*.
26. Hall, *The Unity of the Corinthian Correspondence*, 102–6.
27. Hall, *The Unity of the Corinthian Correspondence*, 199–222.
28. Hall, *The Unity of the Corinthian Correspondence*, 106.

PART I: INTRODUCTION

D. Fundamental Framing Questions

1. The identity of Paul's opponents

It is generally agreed that "No clear consensus has emerged about the opponents with whom Paul had to reckon during the period represented by 2 Corinthians."[29]

Hall writes, "It is clear from 2 Cor 11:22 ('Are they Hebrews? So am I') that Paul's opponents boasted of their Jewish birth. This has sometimes been taken to mean that they were Judaizers from Palestine. There are, however, strong grounds for questioning this view, and for locating their background in Hellenistic Judaism."[30] For, first, there is little trace of the ideas and vocabulary Paul uses to combat Judaizers elsewhere. Circumcision, for example, and the role of the law are not disputed. Second, in spite of Ernst Käsemann's discussion about authorization by the Jerusalem apostles, letters of commendation are not vehicles of authorization. Third, the language about "super-apostles" (Greek, *hoi hyperlian* [superlative] *apostoloi*, 11:15) does not allude to the Jerusalem apostles.

It is probably clearer that the opponents were travelling preachers, perhaps repeating Hellenistic propaganda from Diaspora synagogues.[31] The third chapter (Paul's discussion of Scripture and Moses) is crucial. The gospel ministry, as preached by Paul, is permanent and glorious, in contrast to the "Mosaic" ministry of the newcomers. The written text kills (Greek, *to gramma apokteinei*, 3:6). The enemy is probably not "legalism" here, but blindness.[32] The "veil" is a symbol of blindness. However, apart from Hall's emphatic link of Paul's opponents with Hellenistic Judaism, it is difficult to be much more precise regarding the identity of the newcomers. We know that Paul considered them to be "peddlers of God's word"; preachers of another Jesus, Spirit, and gospel; accusers of Paul as having a weak presence; being manipulators and enslaving people; and being Hebrews and descendants of Abraham.

---

29. Furnish, "Corinthians, Second Letter to the," 225.
30. Hall, *The Unity of the Corinthian Correspondence*, 129.
31. Hall, *The Unity of the Corinthian Correspondence*, 132.
32. Hall, *The Unity of the Corinthian Correspondence*, 139.

INTRODUCTION

2. The tearful letter

In 2 Cor 2:4, Paul says, "I wrote to you out of much distress and anguish of heart and with many tears, not to cause you pain, but to let you know the abundant love that I have for you." The majority view today is that this "tearful" letter was written after 1 Corinthians and is now either wholly lost or perhaps partly preserved in parts of 2 Corinthians 10–13. Hall, however, points out, "Traditionally (and I believe correctly) this letter has been identified as 1 Corinthians."[33] Paul, he argues, was an emotional man, not an academic professor. He adds, "There were many issues discussed in 1 Corinthians that could have triggered such an emotional response" (i.e., as found in the tearful letter), e.g., the party spirit (1:10–13); unspiritual thinking (3:1–3); behaving like kings in Paul's absence (4:8); puffed up with a pride that might require Paul's coming with a rod (4:18–21); the case of incest of which they were boasting; members of the church taking other members to court (6:1–11); consorting with prostitutes (6:12–20); divisions at the Lord's Supper (11:20–22, 27–30); competitive chaos in the "use" of gifts of the Spirit (14:27–33); and a denial of the resurrection (15:2, 12).[34] Hall concludes, Paul's "approach would inevitably have hurt the Corinthians. Many of them were Paul's converts, bound to him by close ties of affection."[35] "The references in 2 Corinthians to a tearful letter are all appropriate to 1 Corinthians."[36]

3. Doctrinal themes

Paul Barnett has helpfully drawn attention to various doctrinal themes in his shorter work on 2 Corinthians.[37] He lists the following, which we paraphrase, with additions:

1. *The promises of God.* God has proved faithful in keeping his ancient promises by his recently inaugurated new covenant of Christ and the Holy Spirit (1:8–20; 3:3–6, 14–18). Moreover, God faithfully delivers and holds onto those who belong to Christ (1:3–11, 22; 4:7–9; 7:6).

---

33. Hall, *The Unity of the Corinthian Correspondence*, 223.
34. Hall, *The Unity of the Corinthian Correspondence*, 224–45.
35. Hall, *The Unity of the Corinthian Correspondence*, 226.
36. Hall, *The Unity of the Corinthian Correspondence*, 235.
37. Barnett, *The Message of 2 Corinthians*, 16–17.

PART I: INTRODUCTION

A promise is not simply a statement but an act. Provided that the speaker is sincere and faithful, in making a promise the speaker commits himself to perform the act which actualizes the promise. For God to make promises to humankind is a supreme act of grace, for God limits his options by committing himself to perform the act which he has promised.

2. *The new covenant.* God has now surpassed and replaced the old covenant (3:7–11). It powerfully meets humanity's needs at their point of greatest weakness, including ageing and death (4:16—5:10), and in their alienation from God because of sin (5:14–21). It is often forgotten that one of the earliest heresies in the Christian era was Marcion's attempt to claim that the Old and New Testaments were not both from the gracious God and Father of Jesus Christ. This devaluation of the Old Testament must always be resisted, and this is affirmed in 2 Corinthians.

3. *Christ is the pre-existent Son of God* (1:19; 8:9). He is the image of God (4:4), the Lord (4:5), the judge of all (5:10), the sinless one who died as a substitute and representative for all people, the one through whom God was reconciling the world to himself (5:14–21). Second Corinthians contains Paul's most comprehensive account of the death of Christ (5:14–21). Here Christology (reflection on the person of Christ) and Paul's doctrine of the atonement (reflection on the work of Christ) are rightly closely integrated together.

4. *The genuineness of New Testament ministry.* This is one of the central themes of this epistle. Authentic ministry is not achieved or validated by letters of recommendation, or by a would-be minister's mystical or miraculous powers, but by his faithfulness in persuading and his effectiveness in bringing people to the Christian faith (5:11–12; 3:2–3). The very existence of the Corinthian congregation was Christ's living letter of recommendation of Paul's ministry. The pattern and measure of the minister's lifestyle is the sacrifice of Christ (4:10–15; 6:1–10; 11:21–23). Establishing true criteria for genuine ministry is one of the major contributions of this letter.

5. *Paul was, both in person and through his writings, the apostle of Christ to the gentiles.* The Risen Lord gave Paul his authority in his historic commissioning of him on the road to Damascus (10:8; 13:10), and Paul's consequent ministry is still exercised to subsequent generations

through his letters, which now form part of the canon of Scripture. This letter is important because it is Paul's major defense of his apostleship to his detractors, whether in the ancient or modern period.

6. *Christian giving and serving.* These arise out of our response to the graciousness of God displayed towards us and in us. Cheerful and generous giving, in all its forms, brings a harvest of great enrichment to the givers. This is seen especially in chapters 8 and 9, which remain an integral part of this epistle.

7. *The Word of God, or the gospel.* This has defined, limited, content, which neither ordained ministers nor anybody else may add to or subtract from (4:2; 11:4). This gospel is exceedingly powerful in bringing rebellious humans under the rule of God (4:6; 10:4–5).

4. Paul: apostle, missionary pastor, and man of intense emotions

In 2 Corinthians, more than in any other epistle, we see Paul bare his soul. He allows us to see his inner self in turmoil. Corinth is the church that he has planted, and he is proud and protective of his converts. When the "false apostles" try to unsettle the church, he becomes understandably upset and even jealous. He has given so much, and suffered so much, but these newcomers make him feel rejected. Their values seek to reverse those of Christ and the cross. Paul feels cut to the heart. What can and should he do?

At times we feel Paul's frustration. The newcomers or interlopers have traumatized him by their arrogance and reversal of the message of the crucified Christ. Nevertheless, Paul's passion is Jesus Christ and his three related callings to be Christ's apostle, a deeply caring Christian pastor, and a missionary prepared to travel and to suffer for the gospel of Christ. In these respects, as Chrysostom has shown, he is worthy of our highest veneration and respect. But this epistle, above all others, shows him as a man, a human being torn by conflicting emotions and inner conflict. The epistle shows us not an idealized Paul, but Paul as he was: a faithful servant of the crucified and risen Christ, but also a human figure. Perhaps we sometimes expect too much of Christian leaders. They are not cardboard saints, but flesh-and-blood servants of Christ, whose thoughts, feelings, and actions we can relate to.

PART II
EXEGESIS

I

INTRODUCTION

1:1–11

1. Address, vv. 1–2

¹ Paul, apostle of Christ Jesus through the will of God and Timothy our brother to God's church which is in Corinth with all the saints who are in the whole of Achaia, ² grace to you and peace from God our Father and the Lord Jesus Christ (Author's translation).

Paul is an apostle because God willed it. Every Christian has a role, provided it is not self-sought but derives from what God purposes. The nature of apostleship will become a central issue in this epistle. In a superb book devoted to this subject in 2 Corinthians, Jeffrey Crafton contrasts apostleship focusing on the *agent* (which the "false apostles at Corinth did) and apostolic agency (which is Paul's way) where apostles become *transparent windows* through which people see only *God in Christ*.[1] As servants of God, are we focused on ourselves or on God, like transparent windows through whom God is seen?

Second, as Paul Barnett argues, Paul declares himself to be "apostle" *by the will of God* in explicit contrast to the false claims of the "pseudo-apostles," whom he specifically addresses in chapters 10–13. There are therefore signs of this major controversy at the very beginning of the epistle. In other words, the theme of apostleship is not a mere appendix or a separate letter but is present from the start.[2]

---

1. Crafton, *The Agency of the Apostle*, especially 63–102.

2. Barnett, *The Second Epistle to the Corinthians*, 59; and Barnett, *The Message of 2 Corinthians*, 24.

Third, Paul is *collaborative*: Timothy is named as co-worker with Paul in five other epistles: 1 and 2 Thessalonians, Philippians, Colossians, and Philemon. He was converted on Paul's first missionary journey at Lystra. Elsewhere in this letter, Silas and Tertius are mentioned. They probably also served as secretaries. The use of secretaries is witnessed in the Greco-Hellenistic world. Margaret Thrall understands "Timothy *the brother*" to mean either "fellow Christian" or "missionary colleague."[3] We noted in the introduction that Paul trusted Titus as his representative to Corinth. Sometimes we must trust others to represent us. A lone, isolated, Christian is a contradiction in terms. As Plummer comments, "the brother" (Greek, *ho adelphos*) means "one of the Christian brothers."[4] Like Paul, all Christians need a church and other people.

Fourth, it has been customary for many commentators to argue that Paul's claim to be an apostle was "to gain authority" (Calvin) or to show that he was "entrusted with authority" (Cerfaux).[5] Yet others, from Chrysostom in patristic times to J. B. Lightfoot, Ernest Best, and many more, have emphasized Paul's "Christ-like weakness" or "feeling of self-abasement."[6] Chrysostom comments, "Here, of him that calls is everything; of him that is called, nothing."[7] There is truth in both sides of this debate. Paul is not authoritarian but reveals his authority through Christ-centered "weakness," especially in this epistle. Other factors about apostleship may be added. "Apostles" in Paul are more than "ministers" because, as witnesses to the resurrection, they are foundational for the church. Paul declares his commission as apostle in Gal 1:1; 1 Cor 1:1; and Rom 1:1 also.

Paul writes to the *church of God*, i.e., the church, which belongs to God (possessive genitive in Greek). This reminds everyone that the church belongs to no individual leader, but belongs to God as his property, which he has saved and redeemed. Certainly "church" does not mean a religious building. Nor is it merely a human religious society (cf. 1 Cor 1:2; 1 Thess 2:14; 2 Thess 1:4).

Further, Corinth is not the only pebble on the beach: Paul writes not only to Corinth, but also to all God's people throughout Achaia. Paul calls them "saints" because God has consecrated or made holy all those whom

---

3. Thrall, *The Second Epistle to the Corinthians*, 82.
4. Plummer, *A Critical and Exegetical Commentary*, 3.
5. Cerfaux, *The Church in the Theology of St Paul*, 25.
6. Best, "Apostolic Authority?"; Lightfoot, *Notes on the Epistles of Paul*, 143.
7. Chrysostom, *Epistle to the Corinthians*, Homily 1:1.

he has redeemed. Every Christian can experience the sanctifying power of the Holy Spirit, whatever inconsistencies and failures may also occur in everyday life. No Christian should forget their privileged status, nor that of other Christians. Similarly, all Christians belong to God, who is a caring and providing Father in a special sense towards those who share the Sonship of Jesus Christ. To sin against a fellow Christian is in this sense like committing sacrilege against God's temple.

In 1:2, "Grace and peace" constitute a conventional greeting. It is a sheer courtesy to use the expected conventions of the day, as Paul did to gentiles (who used "grace") and Jews (who greeted with "peace"). Paul's prayer for "grace and peace" reflects a conventional beginning to a Greek letter, but he fills it with Christian content to make it a genuine prayer.

Questions for reflection

1. Are we like transparent windows through which others can see not us but Christ?
2. Do we try to be "lone" Christians, or are we embedded in the support of a lively Christian fellowship?
3. Do we have an intimate relation with God as our caring and providing Father?
4. Do we prize our status as "saints" in God's sight, whatever our failures and shortcomings?

2. Thanksgiving and hope (vv. 3–11)

Paul follows the address with thanksgiving, as is his normal practice. Many Greco-Roman letters include expressions of thanksgiving. This thanksgiving is in two parts: thanksgiving for God's comfort (vv. 3–7) and thanksgiving for God's deliverance (vv. 8–11).

i. vv. 3–7, Thanks for God's comfort

> ³ Blessed be the God and Father of our Lord Jesus Christ, the Father of mercies and the God of all consolation, ⁴ who consoles us in all our affliction, so that we may be able to console those who are in any affliction with the consolation with which we ourselves are

> consoled by God. [5] For just as the sufferings of Christ are abundant for us, so also our consolation is abundant through Christ. [6] If we are being afflicted, it is for your consolation and salvation; if we are being consoled, it is for your consolation, which you experience when you patiently endure the same sufferings that we are also suffering. [7] Our hope for you is unshaken; for we know that as you share in our sufferings, so also you share in our consolation.

The English word "blessed" (v. 3) is the right translation even if it has become thinned down through overuse. It is characteristic of the worship of the Jews and the synagogue. It means to speak well of, as in the Septuagint (LXX) and Philo. Although it is occasionally used of people in the Old Testament, in the New Testament it is used only of God, which maintains its special use. The phrases "the Father of mercies and the God of all consolation" are descriptive and denote the compassionate Father who is characterized by mercies. "Mercies" (Greek, *oiktirmōn*) is derived from the old verb *oikteirō, to pity*. Paul's address to God as Father reflects Jesus' teaching about God as *Abba*, dear Father. The intimacy that Christians enjoy with God is derived from the Sonship of Jesus, not primarily from God's general good will toward all people. Barnett comments, "It is important for Paul to establish at the outset that God, the God of Abraham, Isaac, and Jacob, was 'the Father of our Lord Jesus Christ.'"[8]

Paul describes Jesus by what is rightly called his favorite title, namely "Lord" (cf. Rom 1:9 and 1 Cor 12:3). In the ancient Greco-Roman world, "the lord" (*ho kyrios*) was the one to whom a slave belonged, but who was also responsible for their care. It was thus a term signifying not only loyalty, obedience, and commitment on the part of the slave, but security and freedom if one had a good lord. Because God or Christ has the care of him, this provides a sense of freedom from self-concern. This freedom arises from the fact that in the event of illness or death, a good lord would care for the slave and his or her family. Rudolf Bultmann writes, "Freedom arises from the very fact that the believer, as one 'ransomed' no longer 'belongs to himself' (1 Cor 6:19). He no longer bears the care for himself, for his own life, but lets this care go, yielding himself entirely to the grace of God; he recognizes himself to be the property of God (or the Lord) and lives for Him."[9]

The God of all comfort (Greek, *paraklēsis*) reflects the Greek word used in John's Gospel for the Paraclete or Holy Spirit, as when some versions

---

8. Barnett, *The Second Epistle*, 68.
9. Bultmann, *Theology of the New Testament*, vol. 1, 331.

translate "the Comforter." It may indicate the lifting of spirits, consolation, or comfort (v. 3).[10] This comforting God "consoles us in all our affliction" (v. 4). "Affliction" (Greek, *thlipsis*) is derived from the verb meaning *to press against*, i.e., *put pressure on*, and means *pressure, stress, affliction, oppression, distress*.[11] "So that we may be able to console" is a regular purpose clause. Barrett comments, "Christian existence, manifested most plainly in the life of an apostle, consists in this paradoxical combination of affliction and comfort."[12] Affliction may qualify an apostle or Christian for ministry to others.

1:5 speaks explicitly of the sufferings of *Christ*. His sufferings "overflow" (Greek, *perisseuei eis*, AV/KJV, *abound*), so that we become fellow-sufferers with Christ (cf. 2 Cor 4:10–11; Rom 8:17; Phil 3:10; Col 1:24). The thought here is the absolute unity between Christ and Christians. Colossians 1:14 even implies that this "supplements" Christ's sufferings, even if Christ's sufferings (Greek, *pathēmata*) are complete and once-for-all. This entails "the fellowship [Greek, *koinonia*, what we share in common] of Christ's sufferings" (Phil 3:10). All who follow Christ must be prepared "to drink his cup" (Matt 20:23). The glorious promise of resurrection with Christ also entails suffering with him. Hughes observes, "Apart from Him, suffering leads to despair, not consolation."[13]

Paul now speaks not only of the Christian's unity with Christ, but also with every believer (v. 6). Our affliction, he says, is "for your consolation and salvation" (v. 6). Whatever the details of the syntax, Ralph Martin observes, "When Paul undergoes apostolic sufferings, it is to benefit the churches."[14] 1:7 explicates the same thought further, adding that his hope for the addressees is "unshaken" or firm. There is a textual variant in the Greek MSS, but both Metzger and Thrall decisively favor the traditional reading as in the NRSV.[15]

Questions for reflection

1. Are we sufficiently thankful to God for all the blessings of life?

10. Danker, *A Greek-English Lexicon of the New Testament*, 766.
11. Danker, *A Greek-English Lexicon of the New Testament*, 457.
12. Barrett, *2 Corinthians*, 60.
13. Hughes, *Paul's Second Epistle to the Corinthians*, 14.
14. Martin, *2 Corinthians*, 10.
15. Metzger, *A Textual Commentary on the Greek New Testament*, 505–6; Thrall, *The Second Epistle to the Corinthians*, 113.

PART II: EXEGESIS

2. Do we think of God as characterized most of all by mercies and compassion or pity?

3. Does "belonging to Jesus as our Lord" relieve us of needless anxieties, or do we seek to carry these as well? Keeping hold of anxieties is not the same as recognizing our own responsibilities.

4. Do the blessings given to other Christians also lift our spirits, whatever our personal situation?

5. Can we see our deep distresses and afflictions as a source of hope?

6. When can we see them as an overflowing of Christ's sufferings?

7. Why can our hope remain firm whatever our failures and disappointments?

ii. vv. 8–11: Thanks for God's deliverance: escape from Asia

> [8] For we do not want you to be ignorant, brothers and sisters, concerning the affliction which befell us in Asia, because we were weighed down exceedingly beyond our own power, insomuch that we despaired even of living. [9] Yes, we ourselves had within ourselves the sentence of death so that we would rely not on ourselves but on God who raises the dead. (Author's translation.) [10] He who rescued us from so very great a death-like experience will continue to rescue. On him we have set our hope, and we still have that hope, [11] while you join in helping us by your prayers so that many will give thanks on our behalf for the precious gift that was granted us through the prayers of many.

This section introduces a major theme, made especially clear in v. 9b, "that we would rely not on ourselves but on God who raises the dead." J. B. Phillips translates or paraphrases this as "We had this experience of coming to the end of our tether that we might learn to trust, not in ourselves, but in God who can raise the dead." Resurrection ranks high in Paul's thought, as 1 Corinthians 15 made clear to his audience, and this verse reminds them.

Paul uses the wording "We do not want you to be unaware, brothers and sisters" (NRSV) six times in 1 Corinthians, 2 Corinthians, Romans, and 1 Thessalonians, to imply that he is giving information that they ought to have known, with also an appeal to their affection and sympathy. Paul now expands on his previous allusion. The distress in Asia is an experience that Paul assumes they know about, but here he expands on particulars. Probably he is referring to persecution by jealous mobs. 1 Corinthians 15:31-32 implies that he was almost torn in pieces, as if by wild animals.[16] In Ephesus, he had "many adversaries" (1 Cor 16:9). Paul and his companions were "so utterly unbearably crushed that we despaired of life itself" (v. 8). He says that he was "weighed down" (Greek, *ebarēthēmen*) beyond the limits of his own human power. "Utterly" and "unbearably" (NRSV) translate Greek *kath' hyperbolēn*, which means a "state of exceeding to an extraordinary degree a point on a scale of extent."[17] Similarly, the Greek for "we despaired of" is a double intensive compound *exaporēthēnai*, where the Greek prepositions *ex* and *apo* both emphasize an utterly exceptional degree of despair.

In the next verse (v. 9), Paul parallels his despair with "received the sentence of death within ourselves." Paul's great trouble had profoundly depressed him. But this was not entirely negative because it taught him not to rely on himself. In the words of Phillips, "We came to end of our tether," or ran completely out of human resources. He thought that his days were numbered. The Greek word for *sentence* or *verdict* was used in AD 51 of a judicial sentence pronounced by the Emperor Claudius. Murray Harris, however, insists that Paul's allusion is to a severe, "painful, death-threatening" *illness*.[18] He cites the frequency of illness in Jewish thought that refers to possible death (cf. 2 Kgs 5:7; Isa 38:16, of Hezekiah). He also compares this with Paul's "thorn in the flesh" in 2 Cor 12:7. He admits that this cannot be proved, but argues that it is very probable.[19] The issue has been sharply debated.[20]

Wilfred Isaacs translates v. 9 as "The fact that we had lost the wish to live was overruled to teach us to trust not in self but in the God who restores the dead to life."[21] Bultmann insists that the renunciation of life is voluntary. He writes, "A voluntary renunciation of life just leaves it to God how he wakens life out of death."[22] He also notes (as Martin does) one of the eighteen Jewish benedictions: "Praised be thou, Yahweh, who maketh the dead alive." But in Paul this specifically relates to the cross and resurrection of Christ.

---

16. Plummer, *2 Corinthians*, 16.
17. Danker, BDAG, 1032.
18. Harris, *The Second Epistle to the Corinthians*, 170-72.
19. Cf. also Harris, "2 Corinthians 5:1-10: A Watershed in Paul's Eschatology," 57.
20. Malherbe, "The Beasts at Ephesus"; Furnish, *II Corinthians*, 122-25.
21. Isaacs, *The Second Epistle of Paul to the Corinthians*, 2.
22. Bultmann, *The Second Letter to the Corinthians*, 28.

PART II: EXEGESIS

Harris relates the consequences of death in 2 Cor 5:1–10. The dead receive "a building from God" (5:1); they dwell in the presence of God (5:8); and they appear before Christ's tribunal (5:10). He adds that we must distinguish between what death is and what it brings.[23] George Guthrie comments, "God has a way of turning desperate situations inside out, turning perplexity to perspective, restoring one's life from the darkest of pits, and granting a sense of purpose to even the most harrowing of life's traumas."[24]

In vv. 10–11, Paul turns to the present: God "will continue to rescue us." The Greek for "rescue" is *rhyomai*, as if to deliver out of a pit. The term "rescue" often features in apocalyptic literature. The verb occurs here in the past and the future with the Greek particle *eti*, "will still deliver." Having shown that there is every good ground for hope, Paul asks for the prayers of the church in Corinth (v. 11). Plummer observes: "These intercessions are part of the machinery which God has provided for preserving His apostle from deadly peril."[25]

This comment is important because it constitutes an antidote to those who suggest that if God wants the best for us, we need not pray anyway because God will do "the best" for us. Edgar Brightman carefully considered this and replied that "the best" is not something fixed and abstract. He wrote, "The best possible when men pray is better than the best possible when men do not pray."[26] In showing how prayer is *part of "the best"* that God wants for us, Brightman also alluded to the role of a praying community, which sighs and yearns with a compassionate heart for the world. Paul likewise speaks of the prayers "of many." Without prayer, there would be no "best." Paul also revels in the thanksgiving of the many for God's answers to prayer.

Questions for reflection

1. Paul's afflictions were such that he even despaired of life itself. Have we ever felt that nothing lay on the yonder side of affliction? Or do we complain even when our affliction is light compared with Paul's experience? Do we expect all paths to be rosy for the Christian?

---

23. Harris, *The Second Epistle to the Corinthians*, 176–77.
24. Guthrie, *2 Corinthians*, 82.
25. Plummer, *Second Corinthians*, 20.
26. Brightman, *A Philosophy of Religion*, 236. Cf. also Brümmer, *What Are We Doing When We Pray?* chapters 5–7, 60–113; and Brümmer, *A Personal God*, throughout.

INTRODUCTION

2. Can "coming to the end of our tether" (Phillips) bring the promise of what lies beyond our human resources? Can we compare this with sharing Christ's resurrection?
3. Do we think of God as One who typically brings life out of death?
4. Do we think of salvation partly in terms of what we have been rescued from?
5. Is prayer an "extra" to be added on to expected Christian practice, or a vital part of "the best" that God wills for us?
6. Do we value the prayers of "many" as expressing the compassionate heart of the wider community?

II

A DEFENCE OF PAUL'S CONDUCT WITH REGARD TO HIS TRAVEL PLANS AND THE OFFENDER

1:12—2:17

This is the first of three sections that consider Paul's recent relations with Corinth in 1:12—7:16. The topics are not as clearly marked as in 1 Corinthians. The sequence reflects Paul's strong feelings. He first insists that his motives have never been dictated by self-interest. Barnett writes, "After writing 1 Corinthians it was necessary to make an unscheduled 'painful' visit (2:1) to Corinth. . . . However, instead of coming back to them immediately, he wrote a letter (2:3; 2:4) and reverted to his original plan to go first to Macedonia and then to Achaia."[1] Some of the Corinthians saw this as vacillation.

1. The theme of boasting or glorying (1:12-14)

> [12] Indeed, this is our boast, the testimony of our conscience: we have behaved in the world with frankness and godly sincerity, not by earthly wisdom but by the grace of God—and all the more toward you. [13] For we write you nothing other than what you can read and also understand; I hope you will understand until the end—[14] as you have already understood us in part—that on the day of the Lord Jesus we are your boast even as you are our boast.

Paul boasts in the testimony of his conscience that he acted out of godly sincerity, not earthly wisdom (v. 12). Furnish translates this as "We can be

---

1. Barnett, *The Message of 2 Corinthians*, 37.

proud of this."[2] *Boast* (Greek, *kauchēsis*) and *conscience* (Greek, *syneidēsis*) are words that Paul has expounded in Romans and 1 Corinthians. In 2 Corinthians, he uses the term "boast" twenty-nine times. "Earthly" translates the Greek word *sarkikos*, which Paul uses five times (e.g.. in 1 Cor 3:3), but which occurs only twice more in the rest of the New Testament. C. A. Pierce argued that conscience in Paul denotes the pain incipient upon doing wrong, but Margaret Thrall has added a corrective that in passages such as this the term also had a more positive meaning.[3]

Barrett reminds us that the great gift of conscience implies man's ability to detach himself from himself and yet view his own character and actions independently. He is thus able to act as a witness for or against himself.[4] Conscience is primarily a witness, as Paul's word "testimony" confirms. It is not, as among most Stoics, the voice of God on ethical issues, for an *uninstructed* conscience is not always absolute or correct. In place of the word *simplicity* some early MSS read *holiness*, partly because the Greek words in capitals look similar. *Simplicity* fits well the context of Paul's defense against the charge of duplicity. God's grace is the alternative to fleshly wisdom.

The contrast between writing and direct presence (v. 13) arises from the accusation that Paul's letters were weighty while his physical presence was less so. The same theme is taken up later. His letters contain no hidden meaning. In the early church, the difference between a tradition of public, rational meaning (as championed by Irenaeus) and a tradition of secret, hidden meaning (as championed by Clement of Alexandria) stresses the importance of Paul's comment. Paul looks forward in v. 14 to the Day of the Lord or Last Day when God acts as Judge and all ambiguities and uncertainties will be done away in God's definitive and final verdict on the truth.

Questions for reflection

1. Are we so accustomed to thinking of ourselves as inadequate that we feel unable to "boast" or "glory" in what God does through us?

---

2. Furnish, *II Corinthians*, 126

3. Pierce, *Conscience in the New Testament* and Thrall, "The Pauline Use of *suneidēsis*"; cf. Eckstein, *Der Begriff Syneidēsis bei Paulus* and Gooch, "Conscience in 1 Corinthians 8 and 10"; cf. also Thrall, *Second Corinthians*, 130–32.

4. Barrett, *2 Corinthians*, 70.

2. What role do we give to our conscience? Do we allow it to be an equivalent to the voice of God, or is our problem the opposite one of repressing it or failing to heed it?

3. People all too readily suspect our motives. Are our motives always pure and disinterested with no thought of self-interest?

4. If we follow traditions or established ways of belief or action, are these publicly debatable, or do they rely on some supposedly secret interpretation?

5. Do we, like Paul, look forward to the day when God will declare definitive truth and dispel all ambiguities? Do we rejoice in God's coming judgment that will not be revised?

2. The postponement of Paul's intended visit (1:15–22)

> [15] Since I was sure of this, I wanted to come to you first, so that you might have a double favor; [16] I wanted to visit you on my way to Macedonia, and to come back to you from Macedonia and have you send me on to Judea. [17] Was I vacillating when I wanted to do this? Do I make my plans according to ordinary human standards, ready to say "Yes, yes" and "No, no" at the same time? [18] As surely as God is faithful, our word to you has not been "Yes and No." [19] For the Son of God, Jesus Christ, whom we proclaimed among you, Silvanus and Timothy and I, was not "Yes and No"; but in him it is always "Yes." [20] For in him every one of God's promises is a "Yes." For this reason it is through him that we say the "Amen," to the glory of God. [21] But it is God who establishes us with you in Christ and has anointed us, [22] by putting his seal on us and giving us his Spirit in our hearts as a first installment.

Paul argues that it was out of consideration for the Corinthians that he abandoned his original plan of coming to see them. He admits in v. 15 that his original plan was to visit them before going anywhere else, i.e., his first plan was to visit them twice: once en route to Macedonia; and second, on his return from Macedonia (v. 16). He speaks of "a double favor" (NRSV), or "to bring you a second blessing" (Isaacs).[5] *Favor* or *blessing* translates the Greek *charis*, which is one of Paul's favorite words for God's unmerited grace and salvation through Christ, although it is here used in the narrower sense of *kindness* or *favor*. He had confidence that they regarded him

---
5. Isaacs, *Second Corinthians*, 3.

as their loyally acknowledged apostle, but subsequently news had reached him that this confidence could not now be taken for granted. For their part, the Corinthians interpreted this change of plan as evidence of Paul's fickleness, insincerity, and unreliability. In v. 17, Paul therefore asks: "Was I vacillating when I wanted to do this?" (NRSV).

If the Corinthians were right, Paul would be making plans "according to ordinary human standards." But Paul flatly denies this. He does not say, "yes, yes" and "no, no" at the same time (v. 17). This would run counter to the faithfulness of God, who is always constant. Had the Corinthians not remained loyal, Paul would have still implemented his original plan. But if he were indeed fickle or duplicitous, this would be like questioning the faithfulness of God, who had called him, and is to be trusted. God's promises stand firm. He elaborates this further in v. 19. Barrett explains, "It is as God's Son that Jesus affirms the being and purpose of his Father."[6] According to Acts 18:5, Paul is joined at Corinth by Silas (Silvanus) and Timothy, and they probably all fell under the same suspicion from some Corinthians as Paul.

Why is Paul so emphatic about God's "yes" and his faithfulness or constancy? From the Corinthians' viewpoint, Paul's saying that he had to do what God wanted might seem to shift the blame for inconstancy from him to God. He is therefore all the more eager to stress God's constancy.[7] Further, God's promises especially to Israel receive confirmation through Christ. Jesus Christ is the "yes" that fulfils these promises (v. 20). In the same verse, Paul says that through Christ "We say the 'Amen' to the glory of God." Plummer notes Paul's inclusion of the definite article in "the" Amen, because this indicates the use "Amen" (May it be so) in public worship, as inherited from the Jewish synagogue and Old Testament (Deut 27:15–16; Neh 5:13, 6, and 8:6; Ps 41:14; Jer 11:5). "Amen" is derived from the Hebrew, '-m-n, suggesting *firmness* or *reliability*.

This leads naturally into v. 21, where God establishes (NRSV) or guarantees (Greek, *bebaioun*) us, with you, i.e., along with you. The verb *bebaioō* occurs often in legal and commercial papyri (i.e., the time of earliest NT MSS). God confirms or verifies both Paul and the Corinthian Christians as his property. There may be a word-play between *Christ* (Greek, *Christos*) and *anointed* (Greek, *chrisas*). The word *seal* (v. 22) continues the theme of belonging to God as his property, for it means preserved intact with a mark

---

6. Barrett, *2 Corinthians*, 76.
7. Cf. Witherington, *Conflict and Community in Corinth*, 363.

of ownership. Sealed goods could not be tampered with, and had their ownership marked in a visible way. Geoffrey Lampe links the seal with the seal of the Holy Spirit.[8] Paul has this link in mind when he continues, "and giving us his Spirit in our heart as a first installment."

The notion of receiving the Spirit as a first installment of more to come is a prominent theme in Paul. Hamilton and others discuss Rom 8:32; 2 Cor 1:22 and 5:5; Gal 5:5; Eph 1:13; and many other passages.[9] The Holy Spirit is both the firstfruits (Greek, *aparchē*) and the earnest, pledge, or guarantee (Greek, *arrabōn*) of more to come. The firstfruits, according to Danker, were the first portion of animals, crops, or dough, of which there was more to come.[10] It is used of people in Rom 16:5, 1 Cor 16:15, and 2 Thess 2:13, and of the Holy Spirit in Rom 8:23 and here. The Spirit is a foretaste of what is to come. Our present experience of the Holy Spirit is only a partial foretaste of the abundant gift that is guaranteed for the greater future. We cannot judge what the future will be like on the basis of the first installment of the Spirit which we can enjoy in part now. The parallel term (Greek) *arrabōn* means "payment of part of a purchase price in advance," or first installment, which exactly matches our modern notion of a "deposit" on a purchase. Both terms imply a guarantee of more to come.

Questions for reflection

1. Are we ever in danger of misjudging the motives of other people, in the same way that some in Corinth misjudged Paul?
2. Are we sometimes, like Paul, willing to change our plans when circumstances change, or can we sometimes be inflexible, for fear of being misunderstood?
3. Is our use of "Amen" in public worship a mere convention or does it express a genuine commonality and endorsement of what has been prayed?
4. Do we regard this situation as reflecting the constancy and faithfulness of God?

---

8. Lampe, *The Seal of the Spirit*.

9. Hamilton, *The Holy Spirit and Eschatology in Paul*, 18–40; Thiselton, *The Holy Spirit*, 73–75 and 84–94; and Swete, *The Holy Spirit in the New Testament*, 192–93, 205–12, and 219–23.

10. Danker, BDAG, 98–99.

5. Do we glory in Christ as the guarantee and confirmation of God's promises to us and to Israel?
6. Do we rejoice in the "seal" by which God has marked us as his property which cannot be tampered with?
7. Do we reduce the confident hope of our future or heavenly experience of the Holy Spirit by measuring it with what we experience now?

3. Whether or not Paul's plans change, his purpose remains (1:23—2:4)

> [23] But I call on God as witness against me: it was to spare you that I did not come again to Corinth. [24] I do not mean to imply that we lord it over your faith; rather, we are workers with you for your joy, because you stand firm in the faith. **2** [1] So I made up my mind not to make you another painful visit. [2] For if I cause you pain, who is there to make me glad but the one whom I have pained? [3] And I wrote as I did, so that when I came, I might not suffer pain from those who should have made me rejoice; for I am confident about all of you, that my joy would be the joy of all of you. [4] For I wrote you out of much distress and anguish of heart and with many tears, not to cause you pain, but to let you know the abundant love that I have for you.

Martin comments that "I call on God as witness" is a mild form of oath-taking.[11] His motive was to spare them, not because of vacillation or faithlessness. There may also be an implication that God knows all hearts. Plummer observes, "There is no sin in swearing to what is true; but swearing falsely is a very grievous sin."[12] The NRSV's "I did not come *again* to Corinth" presupposes that Paul made a second and painful visit to Corinth (cf. the introduction). Many argue that the so-called "severe" letter may perhaps be our present 2 Cor 10–13, written between 1 Corinthians and 2 Cor 1–9.

The next verse (v. 24) is to clarify Paul's meaning. If he has spoken of "sparing" some of the Corinthians, this might be taken to imply that alternatively he could "punish" them. He therefore makes it clear that "lording it over your faith" is by no means Paul's method. Rather, he stresses, he works alongside them (i.e., "we are workers with you for your joy"), so that all may stand firm in the faith. This is one of the few examples in which "the

---

11. Martin, *2 Corinthians*, 34.
12. Plummer, *Second Corinthians*, 43.

faith" is used to denote not simply an attitude of trust, but the whole of our Christian profession of faith.

There is no break in the argument between chapters 1 and 2. In 2:1, Paul continues, "I made up my mind" (NRSV; Greek, *ekrina*, I decided, cf. 1 Cor 2:2) not to come to Corinth again. "If I cause you pain" stands in contrast to "make you glad." *Pain* renders the Greek *en lypē*, which has the sense of "with grief" or "with sorrow," to denote the opposite of *gladness* or *joy*.[13] Plummer paraphrases this as "You Corinthians are my fount of joy; how could I be the one to wish to trouble with sorrow the source whence I draw my own gladness?"[14] Guthrie similarly comments, "Paul notes that if he upsets the Corinthians, there will be no one in the church to 'cheer' him during his visit."[15] The various grammatical forms of the noun *lypē*, sorrow, and the verb *lypeō*, to cause severe mental or emotional distress (passive to experience sadness or distress), occur seven times in 2:1–5. Hall and others emphasize the antithesis between *lypē* and *chara* (joy).[16]

Guthrie renders *lypē* here "emotional turmoil."[17] Paul was determined not to exacerbate an already-difficult situation. He has to reflect how he can confront people whom he loves. Guthrie translates the Greek *ek pollēs thipseōs kai synochēs kardias* as "gut-wrenching and heartbreaking."[18] This expression appears several times in 2 Corinthians, e.g., 2 Cor 1:4, 8; 4:17; 6:4; 7:4; 8:2, 13. It includes turmoil, discomfort, distress, and sorrow. Paul indicates that he wrote a letter "through many tears," i.e., accompanied by many tears, or by a flood of tears.

Questions for reflection

1. Is anything more painful than confrontation with someone whom we love? How does Paul resolve this?
2. Is it just as distressing if someone whom we love misconstrues or distorts our motives? Must this sometimes be the lot of pastors, teachers, or leaders?

---

13. Cf. Bultmann, *Second Corinthians*, 45.
14. Plummer, *Second Corinthians*, 48.
15. Guthrie, *2 Corinthians*, 124.
16. Hall, *The Unity of the Corinthian Correspondence*, 203.
17. Guthrie, *2 Corinthians*, 123.
18. Guthrie, *2 Corinthians*, 125.

3. Does our conscience always testify that every action is performed with the utmost purity of motive?
4. Does our concern for others ever produce "floods of tears"?

4. The need to forgive the one who has caused such pain (2:5–11)

> ⁵ But if anyone has caused pain, he has caused it not to me, but to some extent—not to exaggerate it—to all of you. ⁶ This punishment by the majority is enough for such a person; ⁷ so now instead you should forgive and console him, so that he may not be overwhelmed by excessive sorrow. ⁸ So I urge you to reaffirm your love for him. ⁹ I wrote for this reason: to test you and to know whether you are obedient in everything. ¹⁰ Anyone whom you forgive, I also forgive. What I have forgiven, if I have forgiven anything, has been for your sake in the presence of Christ. ¹¹ And we do this so that we may not be outwitted by Satan; for we are not ignorant of his designs.

In v. 5, Paul says that the offender has caused pain not only to him, but to the whole community. Sin or offence is seldom a merely individual matter. His pastoral sensitivity forbids him to name the man. Barrett and Bultmann suggest that this offence was committed during Paul's painful visit and has no connection with the sin of immorality mentioned in 1 Cor 5:5. They describe it as a personal insult to Paul; the offender "was a stranger."[19] "To some extent" (NRSV; Greek, *apo merous*) is restrictive, i.e., the community was not affected as a whole.

Paul states that the punishment by the majority is enough (v. 6): "So now instead you should forgive and console him" (v. 7). He is not to be overwhelmed by excessive sorrow. The "punishment" might probably have been the withdrawal of fellowship from the Christian community. We may compare how this would be regarded as a punishment with the cavalier attitude that some have toward church attendance and commitment today. In a thoroughly unchristian culture a likeminded fellowship would be close and intimate. They had turned away from the offending brother; now they must turn toward him in love. For "forgiveness" we might expect the common and frequent Greek *aphiēmi* (used 143 times in the NT), but here Paul uses the Greek *charizomai*. This implies forgiving freely as a favor. Free

---

19. Barrett, *2 Corinthians* 90; Bultmann, *Second Corinthians*, 47–48.

grace is always the basis of forgiveness. "Console" (Greek, *parakaleō*) is not "some tranquilizing dose of grace," but "a stiffening agent that fortifies one in heart, mind, and soul."[20]

In vv. 9–11, Paul provides other reasons why he asks for forgiveness of the offender. Paul wanted not only the offender's punishment and forgiveness, but to begin to find out (Greek, *gnō*, ingressive aorist, *to come to know*) if the Corinthians would be "obedient in everything" (NRSV). Barrett suggests that Paul may not be thinking of obedience to himself. At all events, he says that he will forgive those whom the readers forgive, not for his own convenience, or irresponsibly, "but as an act performed in the presence of Christ."[21] Christians who are reluctant to forgive not only forget the extent to which they have received God's forgiveness, but give an advantage to Satan (v. 11), which he may seize and exploit. Paul is content to give advice, not to press his apostolic authority. The NRSV translation is vivid: "that we may not be outwitted by Satan; for we are not ignorant of his designs." Guthrie rightly comments, "Rather than self-centred vindication, Paul is driven by a desire to see a good result for the church, his brothers and sisters in Christ."[22]

Questions for reflection

1. Do we sufficiently realize the consequences that personal deviations can bring for many others? For example, it is often said that marital breakdown or divorce threatens the couple concerned, but children, grandparents, in-laws, and even friends of the couple are also threatened and reduced.

2. Why does withdrawal from the fellowship and support of a church appear to mean so little to some? Is this because our church fellowship has become merely formal and cold or because too many Christians wrongly imagine that Christian faith is a solitary, individual journey?

3. Do we take seriously Paul's concern that Satan can and does exploit our failures to make them have more serious repercussions?

4. Do our relationships become too exclusively personal rather than viewing them within the wider context of the Christian family?

20. Garland, *2 Corinthians*, 60.
21. Barrett, *Second Corinthians*, 93.
22. Guthrie, *2 Corinthians*, 136.

5. Do we try to follow Paul by avoiding naming names, or prefer to "name and shame" at the first opportunity?

6. Is it possible to practice church discipline with such zeal that we almost revel in confrontation? Can discipline be combined with love?

7. Is it perhaps a tribute to Paul's pastoral wisdom and sensitivity that we cannot clearly identify the offender?

5. A further reason why Paul changed his travel plans (2:12-13)

> [12] When I came to Troas to proclaim the good news of Christ, a door was opened for me in the Lord; [13] but my mind could not rest because I did not find my brother Titus there. So I said farewell to them and went on to Macedonia.

Paul now refers to his visit to Troas (v. 12), which would have taken sufficient time for Titus to arrive with news about Corinth. The "open door" makes it clear that Paul visited Troas to undertake missionary work. But he explains in v. 13 that his heart "could not rest" (Isaacs, "was ill at ease") while he was waiting for Titus. He could not be set free from his anxiety (Greek, *thlipsis*) until Titus arrived with news. Chrysostom thinks that Paul would have preferred to stay longer in Troas, but God required him to go on. (Titus appears to have been the first missionary of purely Greek or pagan status. It is possible that if he was Greek, this would have helped his acceptance at Corinth.)

Dieter Georgi suggests that vv. 12-13 continue the theme of Paul's affliction in Asia.[23] But Furnish interprets these verses more positively.[24] Strabo considers Troas one of the notable cities of the world, perhaps of 40,000 people. It was there that Paul had his vision of "the man of Macedonia" who said, "Come over to Macedonia and help us" (Acts 16:6-10); many regard this man as Luke. The "we" sections of Acts begin after this, i.e., when the author of Acts appears to have been a participant in the story he narrates.

---

23. Georgi, *Die Geschichte der Kollekte des Paulus für Jerusalem*, 51.
24. Furnish, *II Corinthians*, 170-71.

PART II: EXEGESIS

Questions for reflection

1. Do we seek God's guidance in our choice of the place where we ought to be? Some Christians may choose where they will live, and then lament the dearth of living churches within reach. What motives govern our choices of travel and place?

2. Troas constituted a watershed in the Acts narrative for advance into Macedonia (Europe) from Troas (Asia). Would Paul have been tempted to make human decisions because an open door was presented at Troas?

3. Paul's experience of anxiety and tension while waiting for news from Titus shows the human emotions of Paul. Does Paul's yearning that all will be well in Corinth suggest how we should think of those for whom we have responsibility?

6. The glory of ministry and God's triumphal procession (2:14–17)

> [14] But thanks be to God, who in Christ always leads us in triumphal procession, and through us spreads in every place the fragrance that comes from knowing him. [15] For we are the aroma of Christ to God among those who are being saved and among those who are perishing; [16] to the one a fragrance from death to death, to the other a fragrance from life to life. Who is sufficient for these things? [17] For we are not peddlers of God's word like so many; but in Christ we speak as persons of sincerity, as persons sent from God and standing in his presence.

It is difficult to decide whether to place a major division after 2:13 or after 2:17. Most commentators begin a new section at 2:14 on the ground that Paul's argument in 2:14-17 is all of a piece with 2:14—7:4. This is no doubt true, but as a matter of convenience we may suggest a division that also allows for shorter sections. Paul's anxious wait for Titus is abruptly dropped and temporarily forgotten and Paul goes on to speak of glorious ministerial triumph in Christ. Windisch calls this outburst of praise a hymn, and Allo believes that Paul's praise is evoked by his mention of Macedonia. Guthrie convincingly brackets 2:14-17 with 2:14—7:4 under the heading of Paul's reflections on authentic ministry.

A DEFENCE OF PAUL'S CONDUCT

Our proposed arrangement of sections does not preclude this. Since the reference to Titus is resumed at 7:5-7, some writers view this as evidence of an editor's piecing together of different letters. The division of 1–8 into fragments has been long held since the work of J. S. Semler in 1776 and of Adolf Hausrath in 1870. Bultmann regards 2:14—7:4 as a separate letter on the apostolic office. Yet this is Paul's rebound of joy on meeting Titus, which also looks back on 2:14-17, and today Margaret Thrall argues for the unity of chapters 1–8.

Considering the meaning of the text, "The major problem concerns the sense in which the verb *thriambeuō* [to lead in triumph?] (v. 14) is used. While it may have metaphorical force, the metaphor must have something to do with the literal meaning of the word."[25] We shall therefore look more thoroughly than usual at this crux of interpretation, which affects the meaning of a triumphal procession. The practice in Rome was to celebrate the triumph of a victorious returning general with a procession in which he would ride in triumph, leading both his victorious soldiers and humiliated captives. This passage almost certainly alludes to "a Roman triumph in which garlands of flowers scattered sweet odors and incense bearers dispensed sweet perfumes. The knowledge of God is here the aroma which Paul had scattered like an incense bearer."[26] But what role do authentic apostles and Christians play when the metaphor is applied? This remains controversial.

Meyer and Denney translate the text as "triumphing over us," which implies that Christ has captured us.[27] Many recent commentators, including Hughes and Collange, also interpret the verb "to triumph" as transitive or causative. But as Robertson and others have noted, there are no known instances of this meaning. On the other hand, as Guthrie points out, the notion of the apostles as defeated captives coheres with 1 Cor 4:9, where Paul observes, God has exhibited us apostles last of all like men sentenced to death, because we have become a spectacle to the world.[28] But controversy does not yet end.

Bultmann provides four distinct possible meanings of *lead in triumph*. Margaret Thrall lists six. Thrall repeats the first possible meaning as (i) that

---

25. Thrall, *Second Corinthians*, 191.

26. Robertson, *Word Pictures in the New Testament*, vol. 4, 218.

27. Meyer, *Critical and Exegetical Handbook to the Epistles to the Corinthians*, 452; and Denney, *The Second Epistle to the Corinthians*, 86–89.

28. Guthrie, *2 Corinthians*, 161.

PART II: EXEGESIS

of the KJV/AV namely "cause to triumph," but comments that the linguistic evidence for this meaning is "weak" or "non-existent." (ii) The apostles can be regarded as sharing in the general's triumph. This makes good sense, but "has no lexical support." (iii) Some stress the "leading about" but without an emphasis on triumph. The emphasis here is on "making visible." (iv) "To make a show or spectacle of" had the support of Chrysostom, and matches 1 Cor 4:9, but risks discarding the metaphor of triumph. (v) Thrall considers something like "subject to humiliation by parading in public." She argues that Paul could have extended the metaphor himself but questions the readers' understanding of it. (vi) She advocates the majority interpretation of it, which celebrates Christ's victory where the conquered display the power of the victor by their status as his slaves. It may further show the graciousness of these prisoners being rescued from subsequent death.[29] Martin relates this to Paul's later self-description as a "pottery vessel" (4:7) to suggest his frailty, while delivering the "treasure" of the gospel message.[30] The clause may still mean "cause *us* to triumph."

Paul's extended metaphor of a fragrance or scent shows that the apostolic proclamation is the medium of universal divine revelation. The perfume spreads everywhere (vv. 14–16), like incense in a triumphal procession. In the Greco-Roman world, fragrance was often seen as indicating the presence of a deity, as in Plutarch. But it may also relate to the scent of sacrifice. This is emphasized by Guthrie, who devotes a number of pages to tracing references to triumphal processions and incense or fragrance in a number of Greco-Roman writers.[31] The scent (Greek, *osmē*) has two opposite effects: that of a deadly fume and a life-giving fragrance. This epistle consistently shows the double effect of gospel ministry. Guthrie expands the "fragrance/fume" metaphor as balancing the allusion to apostles in a more positive way, and concludes, "Paul's use of the triumphal-procession metaphor in 2 Cor 2:14–16a as a whole offers a consistent and balanced word-picture that speaks of the nature of authentic Christian ministry and the effect of this gospel ministry in the world."[32]

"Who is sufficient for these things?" (v. 16c) constitutes a transition to the next section, together with v. 17. Paul is driven to ask this because he has just said that ministers confront the world either with a deadly fume

29. Thrall, *Second Corinthians*, 191–95.
30. Martin, *2 Corinthians*, 47.
31. Guthrie, *2 Corinthians*, 160–73.
32. Guthrie, *2 Corinthians*, 173.

A DEFENCE OF PAUL'S CONDUCT

or a life-giving fragrance. Who can do this? Again, this is where Paul can speak of his "inadequate adequacy." God will qualify him, but not his natural abilities, nor some contrived letters of recommendation.[33] In v. 17 he adds, "We are not peddlers of God's word, like so many." The RSV has "not adulterating God's word," which Thrall endorses. The Greek term *kapēleuō* means "to drive a petty trade," "to trade," or "to peddle," often with a hint of dishonesty. The apostles are not retail dealers. The contrastive term is sincerity (Greek, *eilikrineia*), which may mean either "sincere" or "pure." The authentic apostles are not like the false apostles.

Questions for reflection

1. Are we always ready to give outbursts of praise when we come across instances of answered prayer or of God's special favor and blessing?

2. When the meaning of a biblical passage is not immediately clear, are we tempted to select our "favorite" interpretation over others, or do we patiently wrestle with the text or even consult other people? Do we simply "prefer" a particular interpretation?

3. Do we recognize that authentic ministry may involve hiding under the shadow of our triumphant Lord or do we want always to share his limelight rather than giving to him the whole glory? Can we be like Crafton's transparent windows on 2 Cor 1:1?

4. Can we picture ministers or ourselves as fragile pottery vessels that contain the treasure of the gospel message?

5. Are we alert to the responsibility as Christians as channeling a "pleasant fragrance" or a "deadly fume" to others and the world?

6. Do we sometimes seem to "trade" the gospel, with too much emphasis on "marketing"? Or do we trust God to make his word effective?

---

33. Thrall, *Second Corinthians*, 208–9.

III

THE AUTHENTIC MINISTRY DESCRIBED AND DEFENDED

3:1—7:4

1. Paul's ministry to the Corinthians (3:1-6)

¹ Are we beginning to commend ourselves again? Surely we do not need, as some do, letters of recommendation to you or from you, do we? ² You yourselves are our letter, written on our hearts, to be known and read by all; ³ and you show that you are a letter of Christ, prepared by us, written not with ink but with the Spirit of the living God, not on tablets of stone but on tablets of human hearts.

⁴ Such is the confidence that we have through Christ toward God. ⁵ Not that we are competent of ourselves to claim anything as coming from us; our competence is from God, ⁶ who has made us competent to be ministers of a new covenant, not of letter but of spirit; for the letter kills, but the Spirit gives life.

Self-promotion was the curse of notions of leadership in Corinth. I addressed this at length in both of my commentaries on 1 Corinthians.[1] As we noted in the introduction, Corinth had achieved a remarkable prosperity in commerce and business. This led to a culture of competitiveness, pragmatism, consumerism, and pluralism, which bring us near to the heart of similarities with many Western twenty-first-century cultures. Donald Engels has shown that the prosperity of Roman Corinth rested not primarily upon rents, taxes, and consumer items, but upon its effectiveness as a service economy to tradespeople, merchants, travelers, and those seeking

---

1. Thiselton, *The First Epistle to the Corinthians*, 12-29; and Thiselton, *1 Corinthians*, 9-12.

THE AUTHENTIC MINISTRY DESCRIBED AND DEFENDED

the resources of a well-equipped business center. Services included . . . the availability of imports from a wide range of outlets, both East and West.[2] Many Corinthians experienced rapid or even instant economic and financial success. Ben Witherington sums up the issue when he writes, "In Paul's time many in Corinth were already suffering from the self-made-person-escapes-humble-origins syndrome."[3]

To select only one of many possible examples of self-promotion, to this day the archaeology of Corinth retains the column with an inscription which declared, "Gnaeus Babbius Philinus, aedile and pontifex, had this monument erected at his own expense, and he approved it in his official capacity as duovir."[4] Babbius was at pains to ensure that everyone knew his donation to the city as a benefactor. There is a similar inscription from Erastus: "Erastus in return for aedileship [i.e., public office] laid (this) pavement at his own expense." Witherington observes, "Corinth was a city where public posting and self-promotion had become an art form. The Corinthian people thus lived with an honor-shame cultural orientation, where public recognition was often more important than facts. . . . In such a culture a person's sense of worth is based on recognition by others of one's accomplishments, hence the self-promoting public inscriptions."[5] Wayne Meeks and Gerd Theissen reach similar conclusions. Andrew Clarke shows convincingly that this principle applied most of all to concepts of leadership at Corinth.[6] Stephen Pogoloff shows how this mood also applied to evaluations of rhetoric.[7]

The combined work of Engels, Witherington, Meeks, Theissen, Clarke, and my commentaries proves conclusively that "success" in its crudest form was the key to acceptance at Corinth. In today's language, they wanted only "celebrities." Paul's insistence on *authentic* apostles was the very *opposite* to what they sought, and it took courage and integrity for Paul to point to a way that reflected Christ and his true ministers (3:1–18).

This decisively provides the context for the discussion between Paul and the Corinthians concerning "letters of commendation." In Paul's

---

2. Engels, *Roman Corinth*, throughout, especially 43–65.
3. Witherington, *Conflict and Community in Corinth*, 20.
4. Kent, *Corinth VIII:III, The Inscriptions*, 73; Murphy O'Connor, *St Paul's Corinth*, 171; and Thiselton *The First Epistle to the Corinthians*, 8; it can be seen today.
5. Witherington, *Conflict and Community in Corinth*, 22–48.
6. Clarke, *Secular and Christian Leadership in Corinth*, throughout.
7. Pogoloff, *Logos and Sophia*.

view, "letters of commendation" could be seen to be too close to such self-promotion, and he denies that he is trying to commend himself. All the same, Barrett rightly comments, "The use of commendatory letters was as widespread in antiquity as it is today."[8] Barrett quotes Adolf Deissmann, who cited numerous examples of this from the papyri.[9] Käsemann writes, "Paul defended himself by re-establishing the rules of the game and thereby redefining those eligible to play it."[10] Hafemann affirms this, but adds, "Paul insisted on a 'heavenly criterion' of dependence upon the crucified Lord now risen, which in turn demanded as its corollary a divinely inspired discernment in the Spirit for its evaluation."[11]

A major problem was that whereas so-called apostles in Corinth appeared to have excellent credentials, Paul seemed to lack these and could be accused of manufacturing his own. He asks, "Are we beginning to commend ourselves again?" (3:1). J. B. Phillips renders this: "Is this going to be more self-advertisement in your eyes?" As Harris insists, Paul does not reject all letters of commendation, but he replies that he has no need to do so, as some do, for "You yourselves are our letter, written on our hearts, to be known and recognized by all" (3:2). "Our hearts" is a better attested reading than "your hearts," since Paul regularly associates himself with his readers, as in "We who are left" in 1 Thess 4:17. Paul uses the term "heart" to denote the core of a human person's being, where the Holy Spirit dwells. The Corinthians live as men and women in Christ, the results of the grace of Christ operative in Paul's ministry. *They themselves* therefore were Paul's testimonial, guaranteeing his apostolic status and authority.

"You show" (Greek, *phaneroumenoi*, present participle middle voice, 3:3) may have a passive sense, i.e., you are being made manifest, as Hughes believes.[12] Hughes also points out that this fulfils the prophecy of Jer 31:33, that God will take away hearts of stone to give his people sensitive hearts of flesh (cf. also Ezek 11:19 and 36:26). "Not on tablets of stone" (v. 3) probably alludes to Jer 31:33. The Holy Spirit is in contrast to "ink." This can be discerned, Hughes adds, even amid the shadows of our fallen world.[13]

---

8. Barrett, *Second Corinthians*, 106.
9. Deissmann, *Light from the Ancient East*, 197–200.
10. Käsemann, "Die Legitimität des Apostels."
11. Hafemann, "'Self-Commendation' and Apostolic Legitimacy in 2 Corinthians," 66; cf. 66–88.
12. Hughes, *Second Corinthians*, 88.
13. Hughes, *Second Corinthians*, 89.

Through this living work Paul has *confidence* (v. 4). The construction in Greek emphasizes Christ (Greek, *dia tou Christou, through Christ*), *not self-confidence*. At once he disclaims any originating power for such confidence. It is not (v. 5) from ourselves (Greek, *aph' heautōn*).[14] Isaacs translates, "I lay claim to no qualification but what is God-given."

On the contrary, Paul writes, "Our competence is from God" (NRSV); Greek, also *our sufficiency* (*hē hikanotēs hēmōn*, only here in the NT). Danker translates the adjective *hikanos* as *sufficient*, but the abstract noun *hikanotēs* as *capability* or *being qualified or adequate*.[15] Isaacs continues, "He has qualified me for the service of the new covenant" (v. 6). Barrett rightly comments, "No human being can bear the burden of proclaiming a Gospel that is at the same time 'an odour issuing from death and leading to death, and an odour issuing from life and leading to life.' Only God himself can make men sufficient for such a task. It is this task that is now redefined as that of *ministers* (servants, agents) *of a new covenant*."[16] Isaacs' "he has qualified me" is an aorist tense (Greek, *hikanōsen*), pointing to a definite past act of empowerment at a particular moment, namely the moment of Paul's conversion and call.[17] "Servant" can also have the meaning of go-between, as J. N. Collins has shown.[18] The allusion here to the new covenant looks back to the promise of Jer 31:33, of a new heart.

The new covenant is characterized not by "letters," but by the actions of the Holy Spirit, which also echoes Ezek 36:26–27. Guthrie speaks of the image of "a heart-transplant," and also of Paul's "inadequate adequacy."[19] Of himself, he is inadequate; but as one empowered by God's Spirit he is more than adequate.

The verse "The letter kills, but the Spirit gives life" (v. 6b) has given rise to much controversy over the centuries. In the early church, for example in Origen and Augustine, "the letter" tended to mean the literal meaning of a text. But from the time of the Reformation and Luther the regime of the law was contrasted with that of the Spirit. The regime of the gospel brought life; the law was powerless to do this. This tended to set up a radical dualism.

---

14. Robertson, *Word Pictures*, vol. 4, 220.
15. Danker, BDAG, 472–73.
16. Barrett, *Second Corinthians*, 111.
17. Thrall, *Second Corinthians*, 231.
18. Thrall, *Second Corinthians*, 231.
19. Guthrie, *2 Corinthians*, 192 and 196.

A third approach regards the Spirit as fulfilling what the law required, and thus avoids a radical dualism.

The implied double application of covenant (Greek, *diathēkē*) to both eras confirms this third understanding.[20] "Letter" makes a complete transition from "letters of recommendation," which cannot produce life. Paul elsewhere says that the purpose of the law is to bring life, but human misdirection and self-centeredness make this impossible. It is the Holy Spirit who brings life. The post-Sinai history of Israel is, on the whole, a downward spiral. "Covenant" spells out the terms of our relationship to God as a defined relation that invites trust and confidence.

Questions for reflection

1. Does our church or our broader society encourage a culture of self-promotion, where "success" and competitiveness establish what seems to count in the evaluation of people? Can this lead either to self-glorification or to low self-esteem? Do we expect our leaders or even ourselves to be "celebrities" or "personalities"?
2. Why does Paul so emphatically reject this view? Why is he so unlike Babbius? Why is self-advertisement so alien to Christian faith?
3. Could "a heavenly criterion" (as Hafemann suggests) merely replace one imposed criterion for another? If so, how does Paul avoid this happening?
4. In what sense does Paul have "inadequate adequacy" (Guthrie)? Does he genuinely claim full competency or sufficiency to be a gospel minister?
5. What difference does it make to our evaluation of the letter and the Spirit that both operate within the framework of covenant? Does "covenant" make a difference to the trust or confidence which we are invited to enjoy?
6. What makes a "qualified" minister? Are letters of recommendation (or their equivalent today) always wrong? Can anyone set themselves up as a minister? What credentials are important?

---

20. Guthrie, *2 Corinthians*, 198–99; cf. Watson, *Paul and the Hermeneutics of Faith*, 277.

2. The ministry of the Spirit: Paul's reflection on Exodus 34:29–35 (2 Cor 3:7–18)

⁷ Now if the ministry of death, chiseled in letters on stone tablets, came in glory so that the people of Israel could not gaze at Moses' face because of the glory of his face, a glory now set aside, ⁸ how much more will the ministry of the Spirit come in glory? ⁹ For if there was glory in the ministry of condemnation, much more does the ministry of justification abound in glory! ¹⁰ Indeed, what once had glory has lost its glory because of the greater glory; ¹¹ for if what was set aside came through glory, much more has the permanent come in glory!

¹² Since, then, we have such a hope, we act with great boldness, ¹³ not like Moses, who put a veil over his face to keep the people of Israel from gazing at the end of the glory that was being set aside. ¹⁴ But their minds were hardened. Indeed, to this very day, when they hear the reading of the old covenant, that same veil is still there, since only in Christ is it set aside. ¹⁵ Indeed, to this very day whenever Moses is read, a veil lies over their minds; ¹⁶ but when one turns to the Lord, the veil is removed. ¹⁷ Now the Lord is the Spirit, and where the Spirit of the Lord is, there is freedom. ¹⁸ And all of us, with unveiled faces, seeing the glory of the Lord as though reflected in a mirror, are being transformed into the same image from one degree of glory to another; for this comes from the Lord, the Spirit.

Chapter 3:7–18 can be divided into two parts: the greater glory of the ministry of the new covenant and the Spirit compared with that of Moses (3:7–11); and veiled and unveiled people (3:12–18), as Guthrie broadly suggests. The narrative in Exodus recounts how Moses came down the mountain of Sinai with the tablets of the law, and with shining face. The Israelites were at first afraid to approach him. When he had given the commandments to them, Moses put on a veil. He removed the veil when he entered the Tent of Meeting or tabernacle. He then resumed the veil until he went into the Tent of Meeting again.²¹ Paul expounds this narrative to show by contrast that even if the ministry of Moses was glorious, the ministry of the new covenant is *even more glorious*. This argument by comparison was a typical rabbinic style of argument (technically from the less to the greater).

Paul describes the ministry of Moses as engraved in letters of stone. "Letters" may have a negative overtone, but this ministry is also described as

---

21. Thrall, *Second Corinthians*, 238.

one of glory (Exod 24:16–17; 40:34–35). The Hebrew *kābōd* and the Greek *doxa* (Hebrew and LXX words for *glory*) well convey Paul's notion of splendor, and probably reflect a Palestinian tradition, used, for example, by Philo, a near contemporary of Paul. Yet Paul distinctively argues that this glory was not permanent. The glory lasted for Moses only when he was with God in the Tent of Meeting. The ministry of Paul and the other apostles is a ministry of the Spirit. The two kinds of ministry appear to consist of one, of Moses, that ultimately leads to death and the other, of the Spirit, that leads to life (v. 9). Clearly Paul's theology of the law is not limited to Romans and Galatians. "The righteousness of God," as Barrett comments, refers to God's action in contrast to human action. "Righteousness," further, stands in contrast to *condemnation*, and probably has the added meaning of vindication.

In v. 10 Paul suggests that the glory of the old covenant is scarcely "glory" in the light of the brighter glory of the new covenant, like the genuine light of a candle in the full light of the noon-day sun. The next verse (v. 11) adds another contrast: the old regime is becoming obsolete, whereas the new covenant continues in glory. The old is passing away.

3:12–18 begins a second section about *the veil* (Greek, *kalymma*) and *openness* or *boldness* (Greek, *parresia*). Danker translates *parresia* (v. 12) in three ways that are all interconnected: (i) use of speech that conceals nothing, outspokenness, frankness, or plainness; (ii) openness to public scrutiny; and (iii) boldness and confidence, courage, frankness, as in 2 Cor 7:4 and Acts 2:19.[22] As Robertson points out, the word is derived from *panrhēsis*, to speak everything.[23] The contrast is with the veil that Moses "used to use" or "kept using" (imperfect tense, Greek, *etithei*, v. 13). The Greek *kalymma* means covering for the head or the face.[24] Paul suggests that the purpose of the veil was to prevent people from seeing that the transient glory of Moses actually faded.

This poses two problems for many. Margaret Thrall calls this "a major exegetical problem."[25] Guthrie calls it a debated issue.[26] NRSV has "to keep the people of Israel from gazing at the end (Greek, *telos*) of the glory that was being set aside" (v. 13). Here *telos* is translated as end or termination in a temporal sense. But others argue that the contemporaries of Moses would

22. Danker, BDAG, 781.
23. Robertson, *Word Pictures*, vol. 4, 222.
24. Danker, BDAG, 505.
25. Thrall, *Second Corinthians*, 256.
26. Guthrie, *2 Corinthians*, 239.

not be able to regard this as the "end" of the ministry or covenant of the Mosaic system. They therefore understand *telos* in its alternative sense of *goal* or final destiny, as Harris does.[27] What Moses concealed was the ultimate purpose of his ministry of the old covenant. But, as Thrall observes, this depends on understanding "the Lord" as the pre-existent Christ, "which is debatable."[28] Moses' veiling of himself is to conceal the diminishing radiance of his face. A related problem is whether this implies deception on the part of Moses. The emphasis, however, is upon the veiled response of Israel. The Israelites are cut off or refused access.[29]

This is confirmed by "But their minds were hardened" (Greek, *epōrōthē*) in v. 14. Strictly Paul has departed from Exodus 34, but presumably sees scriptural warrant for this elsewhere. In Romans 11, where he speaks of the "hardening" of Israel, he expounds this theme with reference to Isaiah 29:10. 2 Corinthians 3:14 is reminiscent of Rom 11:8 and Deut 29:4, as Thrall argues.[30] Many Jews of the present day, says Paul, seem to remain as "veiled" as their Israelite ancestors. Jewish resistance to truth, he says, was prefigured in Scripture. In v. 15, Paul says that whenever Jews hear the reading of Moses or the law, "a veil lies over their minds." The theme of the blindness towards God's word was emphasized in the tradition of the sayings of Jesus. This caused Paul great agony of heart (Rom 9:1–5).

In v. 16, Paul turns to the positive. The "veil" is taken away when hearers of God's word turn to the Lord. This (v. 17) is the work of the Holy Spirit. Guthrie comments, "Moses' removal of the veil in the presence of the Lord becomes the foundational word picture to describe the essence of the new covenant gospel."[31] Paul is working towards the section when he says that we see the glory of God in the face of Jesus Christ (4:4–6). Hence, 3:17 asserts, "The Lord is the Spirit, and where the Spirit of the Lord is, there is freedom." Freedom (Greek, *eleutheria*) means especially an open relationship with God, when the veil has been removed. Paul's sentence "The Lord is the Spirit" should not be taken to mean that Christ and the Holy Spirit are identical. Most writers follow George Hendry and Vincent Taylor in regarding "is" as an exegetical "is," i.e., as equivalent to "denotes." Hendry argues that Paul is referring to the meaning of Exod 34:34, where Moses

27. Harris, *Second Corinthians*, 299.
28. Thrall, *Second Corinthians*, 258.
29. Dumbrell, "The Newness of the New Covenant," 78.
30. Thrall, *Second Corinthians*, 262.
31. Guthrie, *2 Corinthians*, 225.

removes the veil when speaking to "the Lord."[32] Vincent Taylor asserts that it means: "Now *kyrios* [Lord] in the passage I have just quoted denotes the Spirit, and where the Spirit of the Lord is, there is liberty."[33] Thrall offers three major interpretations with variants.[34]

The climax of v. 18 is: "All of us with unveiled faces (Greek, *prosōpō*) are seeing (Greek, *katoptrizomenoi*, present middle participle) the glory (Greek, *tēn doxan*) of the Lord, as we are being transformed (Greek, *metamorphoumetha*) into the same image (Greek, *eikona*) (of the Lord) from one degree of glory to another." Every Greek word is significant here. Thrall comments on "being transformed" that this is a "progressive transformation into a condition of glory."[35] All Christians, she says, behold the Lord's glory as though in a mirror. "Unveiled face" stands in contrast to Moses or the Israelites. 4:4 speaks of the glory of Christ, and 4:6 speaks of the glory of God. In Thrall's words, "It is by beholding Christ that believers behold *God's glory*."[36] "The mirror" might denote Christ, who is the image of God, or God in visible form. Another layer of meaning may be found in Wis 7:26, where Divine Wisdom is described as a mirror. For Paul, Christ is God's Wisdom (1 Cor 1:30), perhaps suggesting the mirror image of Wis 7:26. At all events, Christ is the reflection of God, whom we can see face to face. Through this continuous reflection of God through Christ as God's image Christians become transformed.

The account of the transfiguration in the Gospels shows that transfiguration (Matt. 17:2) is linked to moments of revelation. 2 Corinthians 3:18 finds reflection in such passages as 2 Cor 4:6; John 1:14; and 2 Pet 1:18.

Questions for reflection

1. Paul uses the narrative about Moses in Exodus to compare the fading glory of Moses and the old covenant with the permanent and increasing glory of the new covenant through Christ. Can we as readily draw from the Old Testament to enhance what the New Testament tells us?

---

32. Hendry, *The Holy Spirit in Christian Theology*, 24.
33. Taylor, *The Person of Christ in New Testament Teaching*, 54.
34. Thrall, *Second Corinthians*, 278-82.
35. Thrall, *Second Corinthians*, 282.
36. Thrall, *Second Corinthians*, 283 (Thrall's italics).

2. Exodus tells us that the people were afraid to approach Moses when his face shone from seeing God. Do we sometimes take God lightly by comparison, even though through Christ he welcomes us into his presence?

3. The Hebrew for "glory" (*kābōd*) means what is impressive, weighty, and honored.[37] The Greek word for "glory" means radiance, splendor, honor, magnificence, and sometimes worship of a transcendent being. Sometimes Christ's glory is his humiliation in the cross. In Christ, we see the visible *manifestation* of God's presence. Jürgen Moltmann suggests that to glorify God means to love God for his own sake.[38] What do we mean when we seek to give God "glory" in our worship and prayer?

4. Do we tend to give God glory only at times of high spots when we are elated or thankful, and does glory fade at other times as if we were Old Testament people, or is it permanent and progressively increasing?

5. Do "difficulties" in understanding Scripture always relate to insufficient knowledge, or is this ever due to a veil over our hearts?

6. Do we take seriously Paul's warning about "hardening"? Can our hearts lose their sensitivity by overfamiliarity or sin?

7. Does our gaze of Christ lead to transformation into the visible image of God in Christ by progressive degrees "from glory to glory" through the Holy Spirit?

3. A ministry of integrity (4:1–6)

> [5] Therefore, since it is by God's mercy that we are engaged in this ministry, we do not lose heart. ² We have renounced the shameful things that one hides; we refuse to practice cunning or to falsify God's word; but by the open statement of the truth we commend ourselves to the conscience of everyone in the sight of God. ³ And even if our gospel is veiled, it is veiled to those who are perishing. ⁴ In their case the god of this world has blinded the minds of the unbelievers, to keep them from seeing the light of the gospel of the glory of Christ, who is the image of God. ⁵ For we do not proclaim ourselves; we proclaim Jesus Christ as Lord and ourselves as your slaves for Jesus' sake. ⁶ For it is the God who said, "Let light shine

---

37. Brown, Driver, and Briggs, *Hebrew and English Lexicon*, 457.
38. Moltmann, *The Coming of God*, 323.

out of darkness," who has shone in our hearts to give the light of the knowledge of the glory of God in the face of Jesus Christ.

The practical lessons of this short section are many: avoiding faintheartedness, bearing unjust criticism, witnessing to those who have been blinded, preaching Christ and not ourselves, bringing light from God who created light, conveying a great treasure even though we are like fragile earthenware vessels, and much else. Paul begins (v. 1) this section with "therefore" (Greek, *dia touto*), i.e., because the Holy Spirit directs and empowers the ministry of the true apostles, and because they gaze on Christ's glory. For these reasons, "We do not lose heart" (NRSV) or "shrink back" (Furnish; Greek, *egkakoumen*). This verb means *to give in to evil* (Robertson, Greek, *kakos*), *to lack courage, to become weary, to lose heart* (Thrall), or *to lose one's motivation in continuing desirable activity, to be afraid or to be discouraged* (Danker).[39] Paul warns against faintheartedness and timidity when Christians have so much encouragement. The true apostles will not leave a task half done.

In v. 2 Paul expresses the point negatively by saying what "we have renounced" (Greek, *apeipametha*). He states what is alien to his work. Thrall argues that the expression "the hidden things of shame" has no exact meaning. They are hidden things which bring disgrace, not necessarily pagan vices, but probably deceptive communications from the "false apostles." The next part of the verse confirms this: "We refuse to practice cunning or to falsify God's word." "Cunning" translates a colorful word Greek, *panourgia*, craftiness, or unscrupulous readiness to adopt any means to promote one's cause. Guthrie alludes to those who skew the truth to their own ends.[40] Paul's preaching involves "open statement of the truth." Barrett has "we do not adulterate the word of God." This stands in contrast to those preachers who seek "marketing ploys" or bullying tactics to promote audience-pleasing rhetoric (in the ancient world or today), as Pogoloff and Moores have well illustrated.[41] Paul seeks to place the truth before human conscience in all its forms, or "to every man's conscience," "in the sight of God." This provides the climax to a powerful description of authentic apostolic proclamation.

---

39. Danker, BDAG, 272; Thrall, *Second Corinthians*, 110; Furnish, *II Corinthians*, 217; Robertson, *Word Pictures*, vol. 4, 22.

40. Guthrie, *2 Corinthians*, 236.

41. Pogoloff, *Logos and Sophia*, and Moores, *Wrestling with Rationality in Paul*, throughout.

Verses 3–4 show why the gospel seems hidden to some. Paul has said that his ministry is "open," i.e., a public proclamation of the gospel before the consciences of others. So how can some suggest that Paul's gospel is veiled? Thrall suggests that to some of his opponents, it was obscure. To be sure, it concerned a Christ crucified (1 Cor 2:2). Paul replies that any obscurity lies not in the word, but in the *distorted perception* of some hearers. Some are on their way to perdition (v. 3b; cf. 1 Cor 1:23; 8:11; Phil 1:28). 3:4 is more explicit: "The god of this world has blinded the minds of the unbelievers to keep them from seeing the light of the gospel of glory." The god of this world is Satan, who has limited control over the present world order. Barrett argues that this is the devil, and Hughes, Bultmann, Furnish, Harris and Thrall agree with this.[42] There are one or two dissenting voices, however, especially Frederick Long, in a recent article.[43] Long argues that in the Greco-Roman world the title "god" was often given to kings, and Paul is here referring to the Imperial cult. He quotes Bruce Winter as stating, "Paul's greatest enemy in Corinth was the Imperial cult."

Paul repeats that Christ is the image of God (v. 4b). Human beings, as God's image, were intended to show what God is like, but failed to show this image faithfully. Christ alone is the perfect and visible manifestation of God. This was the fulfilment of a task originally given to God's people Israel in which they failed, but it was fulfilled in Christ. The Russian Orthodox theologian Vladimir Lossky argues that by "image of God" we do not primarily mean a string of qualities such as rationality and dominion but the reflection of God as a whole. He insists, "It presupposes grace"; it is not "natural."[44] A person, he argues, is merely an individual by nature, but with the grace of the Holy Spirit he can attain to bearing the image of God in its undistorted form.[45] Most perfect of all, we see the image of God visibly in Christ.

Paul therefore insists that the goal of apostolic and Christian proclamation is to exalt Christ. He makes this clear by stressing that "We do not proclaim ourselves" (v. 5). The more that we understand about the

---

42. Barrett, *Second Corinthians*, 130; Hughes, *Second Corinthians*, 126; Bultmann, *Second Corinthians*, 103; Furnish, *II Corinthians*, 247; Harris, *Second Corinthians*, 327, and Thrall, *Second Corinthians*, 306–9. Others—such as Ford and Young, *Meaning and Truth*—argue that the "God of this world" refers to God himself.

43. Long, "'The God of this Age' (2 Cor. 4:4) and Paul's Empire-Resisting Gospel at Corinth" 221–24.

44. Lossky, *The Mystical Theology of the Eastern Church*, 118.

45. Lossky, *The Mystical Theology of the Eastern Church*, 117 and 121.

"false" apostles in Corinth, the clearer it becomes that they were intoxicated with themselves. Thrall comments, "He is criticizing by implication the behaviour of rival missionaries whose activity (as he sees it) is nothing other than self-promotion."[46] This is also a timely reminder for today when "truth through personality" is used to draw more attention to the self than to Christ. Everyone knows about self-centered ministry where the preacher becomes the sole focus. By contrast, Paul reverses the role to that of "ourselves as your servants for Jesus' sake," while Jesus alone is proclaimed as Lord (cf. 1 Cor 12:3).

Tim Savage in his excellent book *Power through Weakness* singles out 4:6 as the verse in 2 Corinthians that sheds much light on Paul's understanding of the glory surrounding Christian ministry, through which God's gospel light shines in human hearts. He begins his book by showing the concern about social status at Corinth, and in his conclusion calls such an attitude "proud and assertive."[47] He considers boasting in the Corinthian church, and compares glory in the Moses narratives, in Isaiah, and the glory of Christ.[48] The theme of glory through shame reflects the pattern of the cross and the Christian ministry.[49] He provides a good verse-by-verse commentary on 2 Corinthians 4.[50] He argues concerning the attitude in Corinth that Paul "turns its logic on its head," exulting in "the splendor of the cross" and stating the apparent paradox, "When I am weak, then I am strong."[51] The whole book equally expounds 2 Corinthians 4 and challenges wrong conceptions of Christian ministry.

As Bultmann and other commentators argue, "Let light shine out of darkness" alludes to Gen 1:3, in the account of creation.[52] Shining in our hearts, he continues, has nothing to do with Gnosticism or "inner light." The Greek *elampsen* (has shone) is the word that Paul uses in Gal 1:16, where it refers to his call and conversion. Savage, however, argues that it also refers to Isa 9:1 (LXX), "The people that were in darkness have seen a

---

46. Thrall, *Second Corinthians*, 312.
47. Savage, *Power through Weakness*, 19–53 and 197.
48. Savage, *Power through Weakness*, 54–64, 103–29.
49. Savage, *Power through Weakness*, 145–63.
50. Savage, *Power through Weakness*, 164–87.
51. Savage, *Power through Weakness*, 187, 188, 190.
52. Bultmann, *Second Corinthians*, 108.

great light" (Greek, *phōs*).⁵³ Thrall supports this tentatively with "perhaps."⁵⁴ Isaiah and Paul are attacking spiritual blindness. The light of "glory" dispels this. Savage also associates this with Isa 31:17, "You will see the king in his beauty." He considers other uses of glory in the LXX of Isaiah (e.g., Isa 50:10 and 60:1–3). This helps those in Corinth to see that splendor is disclosed through weakness.

Savage states, "It is precisely his [Paul's] humility which authenticates his status as a minister of the glorious gospel of Christ."⁵⁵ This humility stands in contrast to the transcendent power and creative light of God. Thrall links this with Christophany, especially in the light of Acts 9:3; 22:6; 26:13, which recount Paul's call.⁵⁶ She includes an appendix on "Christophany" (the appearance or non-physical manifestation of Christ).⁵⁷ It is possible, she concludes, that Paul regarded his conversion experience when he saw the risen Christ as paradigmatic for others. At all events, the emphasis is on the creativity of God, as in the earlier reference to resurrection (2 Cor 1:9). Guthrie points out that 4:6 is symmetrical with v. 4. "God" matches "the god of this world"; "our hearts" matches "minds"; "the face of Christ" matches "the image of God."⁵⁸ One is negative, with an emphasis on human blindness; the other wholly positive, with an emphasis on God in Christ.

Questions for reflection

1. Can difficulties make us lose heart, and become fainthearted? Are we too easily discouraged by unjust criticism, and risk giving up before our task is finished?

2. Does this kind of difficulty tempt us to go for "marketing" or what pleases an audience or what it expects?

3. How readily do we rely on God and his Spirit to honor an open and honest statement of the truth?

---

53. Savage, *Power in Weakness*, 112–16.
54. Thrall, *Second Corinthians*, 315.
55. Thrall, *Second Corinthians*, 162.
56. Thrall, *Second Corinthians*, 316–17.
57. Thrall, *Second Corinthians*, 318–20.
58. Guthrie, *2 Corinthians*, 243.

PART II: EXEGESIS

4. When we seek to witness to those who seem "blind," do we compassionately realize that stronger forces may have blinded them? Are we aware that we sometimes fight a cosmic battle?

5. Are we committed to manifest the image of God, i.e., reflect God's character to others, or do we thoughtlessly think of "bearing God's image" as a natural and undemanding birthright?

6. How much of our communication is about ourselves, or is our emphasis on the Lordship of Christ, with us as his servants?

7. Are we ever tempted to be "proud and assertive" in the cause of self-promotion, or do we recognize that "power" may come through weakness?

8. Do we see the splendor of the cross in these terms, and base our pattern of ministry on the crucified Christ?

9. Is our trust in God the Creator, who creatively gives light and glory through our weakness?

4. The treasure of the gospel through fragile earthenware jars (4:7–15)

> [7] But we have this treasure in clay jars, so that it may be made clear that this extraordinary power belongs to God and does not come from us. [8] We are afflicted in every way, but not crushed; perplexed, but not driven to despair; [9] persecuted, but not forsaken; struck down, but not destroyed; [10] always carrying in the body the death of Jesus, so that the life of Jesus may also be made visible in our bodies. [11] For while we live, we are always being given up to death for Jesus' sake, so that the life of Jesus may be made visible in our mortal flesh. [12] So death is at work in us, but life in you.
>
> [13] But just as we have the same spirit of faith that is in accordance with scripture—"I believed, and so I spoke"—we also believe, and so we speak, [14] because we know that the one who raised the Lord Jesus will raise us also with Jesus, and will bring us with you into his presence. [15] Yes, everything is for your sake, so that grace, as it extends to more and more people, may increase thanksgiving, to the glory of God.

Plummer admirably conveys the sense of this section. He writes, "It may seem strange that so glorious a dispensation should be proclaimed by such frail and suffering ministers; but that proves that the power of it is from

God and not from them."[59] Thrall states that the weakness and vulnerability of the true apostles was "necessary to the proper conveyance of the treasure of the gospel."[60] The next few verses underline the sufferings of the apostles, who nevertheless carry the unsurpassable treasure of the gospel. We cannot help comparing Paul's metaphor of earthenware or terracotta jars with the Suffering Servant of Isaiah 53, who was despised and rejected yet performed his mission.

Barrett points out that this metaphor is not uncommon, although it was used in various senses.[61] Whether a vessel is made of gold, silver, or earthenware, these may be clean and ready for honorable service. At once, two distinct applications arise from the metaphor. First, the "clay jars" (Greek, *en ostrakinois skeuesin*) underline the inglorious or non-precious nature of the material; second, they point to their fitness to perform some chosen purpose. Guthrie entitles this section, "We are purposeful pots."[62] The Greek noun *ostrakon* means *baked clay*. The phrase was used of all temple vessels (Lev 6:28; 11:33; 14:50). In other contexts, these might be of gold, silver, or everyday material such as pottery. Plutarch describes the triumph celebrated by Aemilius Paulus in which vast quantities of silver coins were carried in ordinary or valueless containers in the procession. The Old Testament has numerous references to earthen jars, of which Paul would have been aware. This all shows that the irresistible or "extraordinary" (Greek, *hyperbolē*) power of the gospel does not originate with the true apostles as such, but with God.

Paul then explains what the "externals" of true apostleship involve in everyday life. In Guthrie's words, Paul capitalizes on a common aspect of everyday life. Clay jars were unexceptional, affordable, disposable, and mass-produced. In 4:8-9, Paul begins his list of hardships: afflicted, perplexed, persecuted, struck down (vv. 8-9, NRSV). These are like Paul's "catalogue of afflictions" in 1 Cor 4:8-13. They have received careful examination by Fitzgerald, Hafemann, Hodgson, Kleinknecht, Plank, Schrage, and others.[63] The major difference between 1 Cor 4 and 2 Cor 4, however, is the pairing

59. Plummer, *Second Corinthians*, 122-23.
60. Thrall, *Second Corinthians*, 324.
61. Barrett, *Second Corinthians*, 137.
62. Guthrie, *2 Corinthians*, 232.
63. Fitzgerald, *Cracks in an Earthen Vessel*, 1988, especially 117-48; Hafemann, *Suffering and the Spirit*, especially 58-64; Hodgson, "Paul the Apostle and First Century Tribulation Lists"; Kleinknecht, *Der leidende Gerechtfertigte*, 208-304; Plank, *Paul and the Irony of Affliction*, especially 33-70; Schrage, "Leid, Kreuz und Eschaton."

of the concepts in dialectic (i.e., contrast): afflicted (Greek, *thlibomenoi, restricted, pressed*) but not crushed (Greek, *ou stenochōroumenpoi*); perplexed but not driven to despair (or driven to desperation, Greek, *exaporoumenoi*, with intensive [i.e., emphatic] *ek* or *ex*); persecuted but not forsaken; struck down but not destroyed (i.e., knocked down, but not left for dead). Thrall comments that this last pair may reflect a soldier's experience of being felled to the ground but struggling to one's feet again.[64] Guthrie comments, "all of the participles describing the challenges of those involved in Paul's ministry are present tense in form, indicating that Paul has in mind common ongoing experiences, and thus are 'customary' uses of the present tense."[65] He adds, "The difficulties surrounding his ministry go with the territory."

In 4:10–13, Paul specifically associates his sufferings with the death of Jesus, that the life of Jesus may also be made visible in our bodies (v. 10). Thrall rightly calls it "a Christological interpretation of the experiences described in the participles in the antitheses of 8–9."[66] "The death" (Greek, *tēn nekrōsin*, not *ton thanaton*, plural, literally the puttings to death, or deadnesses) means either putting to death as a *process* (Barrett, Hughes) or deadness as a *state*, the state of death (Furnish). It means the latter in Rom 4:19. Some regard this as suffering as Jesus suffered. But the language of following in the sense of imitation is not frequent in Paul. Others refer to the baptismal dying with Christ in Rom 6:3. Or it may be that the apostolic suffering is an earthly manifestation of the gospel. The life of Jesus does not mean his earthly life, but the power of his resurrection life (Furnish).[67] It is "God's power taking shape in the form it took in the resurrection of Jesus."[68] "Always" carrying about (Greek, *peripherontes*) the dying refers to the constant threat under which the apostle ministers (Guthrie).[69] Isaacs renders this verse "We accept death as readily as the Lord Jesus accepted it," which is clear in meaning but hardly conveys Paul's deepest theology of union with Christ, although he does deepen it by speaking of Christ's death and resurrection being "clearly reproduced."[70]

---

64. Thrall, *Second Corinthians*, 330; cf. 326–31.
65. Guthrie, *2 Corinthians*, 255.
66. Thrall, *Second Corinthians*, 331.
67. Furnish, *II Corinthians*, 256.
68. Thrall, *Second Corinthians*, 335.
69. Guthrie, *2 Corinthians*, 259.
70. Isaacs, *Second Corinthians*, 9–10.

THE AUTHENTIC MINISTRY DESCRIBED AND DEFENDED

The next verse (v. 11) is largely an explanatory repetition of v. 10. Isaacs renders it "We are delivered up to death for Jesus' sake, . . . our deliverances show forth his triumph over death."[71] The NRSV helpfully renders part of v. 11: "that the life of Jesus may be made visible in our mortal flesh"; i.e., just as Jesus as God's image made God *visible* through his incarnation or enfleshment, so the apostles make Christ *visible* through their everyday life and behavior. It is well known that Albert Schweitzer perceived this in a literal and mystical way. He wrote, "Dying and rising with Christ is for him [Paul] not something merely metaphorical. . . . For him the believer experiences the dying and rising again of Christ in actual fact."[72]

Schweitzer unfortunately made this "mystical" dying and rising an *alternative* to Paul's concept of justification by grace through faith. He also grossly overstated this "mystical" approach, and it has lost favor in Pauline scholarship. It is more customary today to speak of "participation in Christ."[73] Dunn describes this as "the sense of being bound up with Christ," which has a definite beginning and an ongoing relation. He finds this in Rom 6:3-8; 5:12-21; 1 Cor 12:13; Gal 2:19-20; Phil 3:8-11; and elsewhere.[74] Earlier, this approach can be found in L. S. Thornton and many others.[75] Paul concludes the death-and-life theme in v. 12: "So death is at work in us, but life in you"; i.e., Paul's ministry functions as the means by which the Corinthians have experienced the gospel life of Jesus.[76] Barrett compares this with Col 1:24, where Paul endures "what is left over of the Messianic afflictions," though not implying that Christ's suffering was not complete and "finished."[77]

Paul returns to the theme of life, confidence, faith, and belief in vv. 12-15. The immediate connection of v. 13 with the previous section may not be obvious, for Margaret Thrall lists five attempted explanations of the logical link. She concludes that "We have" (Greek has the participle, *echontes*) has causal force, providing the grounding for "We believe" (with Furnish, Barrett, and Plummer). Although the NRSV renders "spirit of faith," Thrall rightly argues that spirit may allude to the Holy Spirit, which would connect

---

71. Isaacs, *Second Corinthians*, 10.
72. Schweitzer, *The Mysticism of Paul the Apostle*, 15-16; 96-97; 115-16.
73. Cf. Dunn, *Theology of Paul the Apostle*, 390-412.
74. Dunn, *Theology of Paul the Apostle*, 410-11.
75. Thornton, *The Common Life in the Body of Christ*, throughout.
76. Guthrie, *2 Corinthians*, 261.
77. Barrett, *Second Corinthians*, 142.

well with the quotation from the inspired psalmist in Ps 115:1 (LXX; Heb. Ps 116:10), "I believed, and so I spoke."[78] (This is one of several points at which the NRSV renders the Hebrew or Greek as "spirit" rather than "Spirit.") For Paul, "I spoke" alludes to the preaching of the gospel.[79] The Scriptures vindicate preaching on the basis of faith.[80]

The next verse (4:14) focuses on a theology of resurrection as providing Paul with confidence while he faces the threat of death.[81] His wording "We know that the one who raised the Lord Jesus will raise us also with Jesus" strongly anticipates Rom 8:11: "He who raised Christ from the dead will give life to your mortal bodies also through his Spirit that dwells in you." It also looks back to 1 Thess 4:17, 1 Cor 15:52, and 2 Cor 12:9-11. Like 2 Cor 1:9, it probably refers both to the future promise of resurrection at the coming of Christ and the restorative power of God to revive us to life now. This coheres with a strong eschatology that also affirms fulfilment in process of present realization. Harris argues that "with Jesus" means "in the wake of" rather than "at the same time as," as Plummer, Bruce, and Guthrie, also note.[82]

Paul gives a further reason for perseverance and confidence in v. 15. He goes forward "for your sake," and that "more and more people may increase thanksgiving to the glory of God" (NRSV). Furnish describes v. 15b as "a syntactical thicket," to which he suggests three possible ways forward, even if the construction remains problematic.[83] Most English versions resort to paraphrase and treat "increase" (Greek, *pleonazein*) as intransitive; while others treat it as transitive with "thanksgiving as its object. Thrall is more positive. She asserts that "the basic point is clear," even if details of interpretation vary: "The thought is that grace, having increased its influence through the response of more and more people, will cause an increase of thanksgiving, to the glory of God."[84] "Grace" is the gracious divine power at work in the hearts and lives of the readers. Increase and abundance are characteristic words in 2 Corinthians.[85] As Paul goes on, the grace of God makes its impact, in spite of hardships or through them.

---

78. Thrall, *Second Corinthians*, 338-39.
79. Furnish, *II Corinthians*, 258.
80. Guthrie, *2 Corinthians*, 262.
81. Guthrie, *2 Corinthians*, 263.
82. Harris, *Second Corinthians*, 253.
83. Furnish, *II Corinthians*, 259-60.
84. Thrall, *Second Corinthians*, 344.
85. Young and Ford, *Meaning and Truth in 2 Corinthians*, throughout.

Questions for reflection

1. If we often feel as fragile as earthenware jars, do we still feel a sense of purpose and that costly and valuable commodities can still be conveyed by very ordinary receptacles?
2. Do we realize that the very ordinariness of the containers constitutes a necessary part of the gospel design?
3. Do we imagine that "hardships" and "afflictions" are things from which Christians and Christian ministers should expect to be exempt, or do we see them as a stamp of authenticity? Do we relate them to Paul's "catalogue of hardships" in 1 Cor 4:8–13 and 2 Cor 4?
4. Can we relate these experiences to participation in Christ's afflictions? Do we both complain and also shrink from aspiring to this sign of union with Christ? Can our bearing afflictions be a way of making Christ visible in everyday life?
5. Do we, like the Suffering Servant of Isaiah, regard this as a way of bringing life to others?
6. Do we too easily relegate "belief" to the merely intellectual side of life? Is right belief the basis of our speaking or preaching?
7. Do we regard God's gift of resurrection as both a confident future hope and a present restorative revival in the present (as in 2 Cor 1:9)?
8. Do we see the ongoing progress of the gospel as a divine power that evokes thanksgiving from more and more people?

5. The present and the future as seen and unseen: longing to be clothed (4:16—5:10)

[16] So we do not lose heart. Even though our outer nature is wasting away, our inner nature is being renewed day by day. [17] For this slight momentary affliction is preparing us for an eternal weight of glory beyond all measure, [18] because we look not at what can be seen but at what cannot be seen; for what can be seen is temporary, but what cannot be seen is eternal.

5 For we know that if the earthly tent we live in is destroyed, we have a building from God, a house not made with hands, eternal in the heavens. [2] For in this tent we groan, longing to be clothed with our heavenly dwelling— [3] if indeed, when we have taken it off we will not be found naked. ⁴ For while we are still in this tent, we groan under our burden, because we wish not to be unclothed but to be further clothed, so that what is mortal may be swallowed up by life. ⁵ He who has prepared us for this very thing is God, who has given us the Spirit as a guarantee.

⁶ So we are always confident; even though we know that while we are at home in the body we are away from the Lord— ⁷ for we walk by faith, not by sight. 8 Yes, we do have confidence, and we would rather be away from the body and at home with the Lord. ⁹ So whether we are at home or away, we make it our aim to please him. ¹⁰ For all of us must appear before the judgment seat of Christ, so that each may receive recompense for what has been done in the body, whether good or evil.

It is not always easy for Western minds, which are accustomed to make *spatial* distinction between the material and invisible worlds, to see that Hebrew, Jewish, and early Christian thought often made this distinction in terms of the *temporal* contrast between the present (seen or material) realm and that of the future (eternal) realm. Oscar Cullmann famously wrote, "Primitive Christian faith and thinking do not start from the spatial contrast between the Here and the Beyond, but from the time distinction between the . . . Now and Then. In saying this we do not mean that the mainly spatial contrast between visible and invisible does not here exist," but "the essential thing is not the spatial contrast, but the distinction which faith makes between the times."[86] In this present section, therefore, there is an intimate connection between Paul's language about our outer nature and inner nature (v. 16), the momentary affliction and an eternal weight of glory (v. 17), and what is seen and what cannot be seen and the temporary and eternal (v. 18). This is underlined by 5:1, on the hope for a building from God "eternal in the heavens."

Plummer paraphrases "No wonder that we do not lose heart" (v. 16). The destruction of the outward self is clearly connected with the description of apostolic suffering in vv. 7–12. But the reference to future eternal glory and the eternal unseen realities leads to the theme of the future in 5:1–10. The contrast between the inner and outer man appears in Paul for the first time in the Corinthian correspondence. Jewett takes the "inner man" to refer to the heart.[87] Thrall rightly insists that both terms refer to the *whole* person: the whole person as seen by others from without; and

---

86. Cullmann, *Christ and Time*, 37.
87. Jewett, *Paul's Anthropological*, 397.

the whole self as visible only to God.[88] She adds that the "outward man" of 2 Cor 4:16 is to be identified with the "old man" of Rom 6:6. Inward renewal is set over against outward degeneration.

As Bultmann argues, the inward man is "not the life of the human spirit."[89] Paul does not depend on Hellenistic dualism here. The point is that from the perspective of outward appearances Paul and his mission may not seem to be going well, but this is no reason for discouragement. Paul appeals to the existence of another world, like Elisha's vision of the heavenly horses and chariots of fire that surrounded the Syrians.[90] Only in Paul these two worlds are not contrasted spatially but temporally. We recall some words from A. P. Hogg: "There is a kingdom where . . . children play with infinite forces, where the child's little finger becomes stronger than the giant world: a wide kingdom where the world exists only by sufferance: to which the world's laws of development are forever subjected: in which the world lies like a foolish, wilful dream in the solid truth of the day."[91]

In the light of all this Paul is encouraged to persevere. His different perspective expresses the Christian hope and confidence. The experience of wasting away (Greek, *diaphtheiretai*) in terms of externals and physical existence does not have the last word. Hence, "On the contrary we do not give up." In v. 17, Paul substantiates what he has just said. The eternal glory that results from affliction motivates his perseverance in his apostolic duty. His affliction has been "light" or "insignificant" (Greek, *elaphron*) compared with the "weight" (Greek, *baros*) of the glory that is coming. Affliction is relatively a "light bundle."[92]

4:18 expounds Paul's famous contrast between what is "seen" and temporary and what is "unseen" and eternal. His new perspective is "before God." He is primarily orientated to the spiritual realm as God sees it. Some translations render this as "We do not focus on what is seen" (NIV; TNIV; Holman Christian Standard Bible; and New Living Translation). The main point is not that affliction is light, but that it produces glory.[93]

5:1–10: The supposed change of theme in 5:1–10 is not a genuine change at all, in the light of the comment of Cullmann and others about the

---

88. Thrall, *Second Corinthians*, 350.
89. Bultmann, *Second Corinthians*, 125.
90. Guthrie, *2 Corinthians*, 269.
91. Hogg, *Redemption from this World*, 25–26.
92. Danker, BDAG, 314; Guthrie, *2 Corinthians*, 271.
93. Thrall, *Second Corinthians*, 355.

temporal distinction between the present and the future. Isaacs paraphrases 5:1 as "This body that we live in on the earth is but a tent (Greek, *skēnos*), and we know that if the tent be taken down, there awaits us in the heavens a permanent building, God's gift to us, a dwelling built by no human hand, and destined to endure for ever."[94]

The complexity of the interpretation of 5:1 is indicated by Thrall's devoting thirteen pages to the exegesis of this verse, Harris spending a similar space, and Allo some twenty pages on the history of its interpretation. Barrett calls it "notoriously difficult."[95] Yet Paul begins with a confident "We know" (Greek, *oidamen*) on the basis of apostolic eyewitnesses (1 Cor 15:3–8) and personal experience of the risen Christ. "We know that if the earthly tent we live in is destroyed (Greek, *hē epigeios hēmōn oikia tou skēnous kataluthē*), we have a building (Greek, *oikodomēn*) from God, a house not made with hands, eternal in the heavens" (NRSV). *Tent* suggest impermanence and insecurity. Superficially this seems to reflect the Greek notion of a temporary body for the soul, but Barrett and J. N. Sevenster rightly reject any affinity with Hellenism in Paul. "Made with hands" is used by Paul and by Stephen in Acts 7:48 to denote the merely human. The word which the NRSV renders "destroyed" means "dismantled."

By contrast, the "building" is from God, "not made with hands." Most commentators understand this to refer to the resurrection body, which Paul has already defined in 1 Cor 15:44–45. This is what God alone can do.[96] Paul has expounded this in 1 Cor 15:32–57, and earlier in 1 Corinthians as a whole. Karl Barth has made this clear.[97] He wrote, "This 'of God' is clearly the secret nerve of this whole (epistle)."[98] Plummer suggests that *oikodomē* (building) is "the building *process*, which results in an edifice."[99]

Of the many exegetical problems of 5:1–4, does Paul's concept of "being naked" (v. 3) suggest an intermediate state, or period between the death of a Christian and their putting on of the spiritual body at the parousia? Martin comments that "There is no consensus."[100] A second problem is whether this section represents a change in Paul's eschatology from earlier

---

94. Isaacs, *Second Corinthians*, 11.
95. Barrett, *Second Corinthians*, 150; Allo, *Seconde épitre aux Corinthiens*.
96. Guthrie, *2 Corinthians*, 278.
97. Barth, *The Resurrection of the Dead*, 17–20.
98. Barth, *The Resurrection of the Dead*, 18.
99. Plummer, *Second Corinthians*, 141 (his italics).
100. Martin, *2 Corinthians*, 97.

epistles. C. H. Dodd and W. L. Knox were advocates of this view.[101] Does this imply that Christians receive their spiritual body at death? Barrett rejects this view, and J. Lowe has shown that Paul maintains the same eschatology over the years of his life.[102]

In any case, notions of "the intermediate state" are based on a misunderstanding. The philosopher Gilbert Ryle has convincingly revealed the key difference between a "participant" viewpoint and a "descriptive" or "observer" one. He illustrates this from the great paradoxes of ancient Greek philosophy.[103] But we can suggest the homely illustration of trying to explain Christmas morning to a child. From the participant's viewpoint, it is correct to say that the sooner the child falls asleep, the sooner Christmas will be here. But from the observer's viewpoint, much has to happen between the child's falling asleep and the arrival of Christmas morning. Presents may have to be wrapped; people may want to go to Midnight Communion. In the same way, the dying Christian, from the participant's viewpoint, may know nothing before waking up with Christ. But from an observer's or theologian's viewpoint, much has first to happen: the parousia or future coming of Christ, the last judgment, and the final resurrection. Paul does not need to abandon the observer viewpoint of 1 Thessalonians and 1 Corinthians in order to express perhaps the participant's viewpoint of 2 Corinthians. He asserts both: the careful eschatology of 1 Corinthians, side by side with "to depart and be with Christ" in Phil 3:23.

One other well-known difficult interpretation is that of E. Earle Ellis, which he proposed in 1960.[104] Ellis understands the "building" of God to refer to corporate identity of the community of believers, in contrast to the Jewish temple. It would therefore not allude to the individual believer's experience at death. The "nakedness" of 5:3 does not refer to being without a body, but the shameful condition of being without Christ. But Hafemann has criticized this view, and in general it does not seem to be taken up by most commentaries.[105]

In vv. 2–5, Paul addresses the groaning (Greek, *strenazō*) of earthly existence compared with the glory of the resurrection and "our habitation in heaven." The Greek *strenazō* means to sigh or to groan. In contrast to

---

101. Knox, *Paul and the Church of the Gentiles*, 121–45; Dodd, "The Mind of Paul."
102. Lowe, "An Attempt to Detect Developments in St. Paul's Eschatology."
103. Ryle, *Dilemmas*, 1–81.
104. Ellis, "II Corinthians V:1–10 in Pauline Eschatology."
105. Martin, *2 Corinthians*, 99–100, and Guthrie, *2 Corinthians*, 275, n.3.

this, Paul longs for the resurrection body. He uses a vivid metaphor of putting clothing on over (Greek double compound, *ependysasthai, to put on over*). Guthrie and Belleville suggest that the immortal body is put on "as an imperishable topcoat."[106] Behind this metaphor, however, the housing imagery remains. The Greek *oikētērion* is a dwelling or habitation, which is more permanent than a tent. It is in harmony with 1 Cor 15:53: "This perishable body must put on imperishability, and this mortal body must put on immortality."

Verse 3 introduces a debated point, with its conditional "if indeed, when we have taken it off." Thrall suggests that the conditional leaves room for the possibility that the parousia, or future coming of Christ, may occur even before the Christian dies.[107] This would cohere with 1 Thess 4:17, where Paul says, "*We* who are alive, who are left . . . ," because if he had said "*They* who are alive . . . ," this would suggest to his readers that Paul did not take the possible arrival of the parousia during their life time seriously. As the philosopher P. F. Strawson points out, there is all the difference in the world between an assertion and a conditional presupposition.[108]

This does not commit Paul to the belief that the parousia *will* happen in his lifetime but simply allows for the *possibility*. After all, even Jesus said that of that time, no one knows, not even the Son, but the Father (Mark 13:32). Thrall also points to several senses in which interpreters have understood the word "naked."[109] Some refer to the state of the soul when it is stripped from the body, i.e., disembodied. But Paul does not normally use the term "soul" in this way. Others use the term as a sign of shame, to denote those who are guilty before God, i.e., moral nakedness. In the end, after a long discussion, Thrall argues that the grammar suggests an unfulfilled hypothesis. Guthrie suggests the term "inadequately dressed."[110] Plummer thinks that the general meaning is that "Life here is only a pilgrimage." Christians are citizens of a realm that is in heaven, and on earth they are only sojourners."[111]

C. F. D. Moule and George Guthrie argue that even if humans prefer the "addition" of the resurrection body, i.e., "putting on over," God chooses

---

106. Guthrie, *2 Corinthians*, 280 and Belleville, *2 Corinthians*, 134.
107. Thrall, *Second Corinthians*, 376–77.
108. Strawson, *An Introduction to Logical Theory*, 175–79.
109. Thrall, *Second Corinthians*, 376–79.
110. Guthrie, *2 Corinthians*, 282.
111. Plummer, *Second Corinthians*, 142.

transformation and exchange. Guthrie points out, "The resurrection does not involve a mere laying aside of one body for another.... Rather, in the resurrection the earthly body is transformed, swallowed up, in the process of resurrection."[112] This echoes 1 Cor 15:54, where death is "swallowed up in victory." Whatever the diminishing capacities of the earthly body, this is part of God's plan for the resurrection transformation.

In 2 Cor 5:5, Paul expresses his confidence not only in God who raises the dead (1:9), but also in the Holy Spirit, who is the agent of the resurrection. The Spirit, Guthrie rightly comments, "formed a cornerstone of eschatology."[113] This verse includes the well-known reference to the "guarantee" or seal of the Spirit. "Guarantee" translates the Greek *arrabōn*, which Danker calls "the payment of part of a purchase price in advance; first installment, deposit, down payment, pledge."[114] Paul uses the same term in Rom 8:22–23, where it is often translated "the firstfruits" of the Holy Spirit, i.e., the first installment of more which is to come. The KJV/AV has "earnest of the Spirit." It is a pledge of more of the same quality to come. Hermann Gunkel and Neill Hamilton emphasize this aspect. Hamilton writes, "The centre of gravity lies in the future.... 'He who sows to the Spirit will of the Holy Spirit reap eternal life' (Gal 6:8)."[115] We often measure the power of the Spirit by what we experience now, but Paul affirms that what we see now is a mere fraction of what we shall see in our resurrection and post-resurrection experience.

2 Corinthians 5:6–8 begins a second subsection of 2 Cor 5:1–10. Paul begins "We are confident" and speaks of being "at home" in the body and "away" from the Lord. Life here on earth (*being at home*, Greek, *endēmeō*) involves a relative "being away" (Greek, *ekdēmeō*) from the Lord. Life in this world means a kind of exile.[116] Verse 7 amplifies what he has said in v. 6: the presence of God in Christ is apprehended by faith, not sight. Faith does not mean a blind leap in the dark but constitutes a positive attitude of appropriation. Elsewhere, I have distinguished thirteen meanings of "faith" in the New

---

112. Guthrie, *2 Corinthians*, 283.
113. Guthrie, *2 Corinthians*, 284.
114. Danker, BDAG, 134.
115. Hamilton, *The Holy Spirit and Eschatology in Paul*, 19; cf. Gunkel, *The Influence of the Holy Spirit*, 82; and Thiselton, *The Holy Spirit*, 73.
116. Thrall, *Second Corinthians*, 386.

Testament.[117] Sometimes, as here, faith involves belief and trust.[118] Martin Luther once defined faith as "a living, daring, confidence in God's grace, so sure and certain that a man would stake his life on it a thousand times. This confidence in God's grace . . . makes men glad and bold and happy."[119] This reflects Paul's allusion to confidence in 5:8.

In 5:9–10, Paul underlines our accountability to God. This remains the case whether we are at home or away. He has been thinking of the future resurrection and therefore his mind moves to what is inextricably tied to it, namely the last judgment, or the tribunal of Christ. Every person, including every Christian, will face this. But it would be wrong to think of the judgment as being like an appearance before a heavenly headmaster, who awards verdicts of merit or demerit. To be sure, Paul says, "All of us must appear before the judgment seat of Christ, so that each may receive recompense for what has been done in the body, whether good or evil" (v. 10). But in the Old Testament the prospect of judgment is a cause of joy, not fear or anxiety. Why is this so?

The Psalmist writes, "He [God] will judge the peoples with equity. Let the heavens be glad, and the earth rejoice. . . . Then shall all the trees of the forest sing for joy before the LORD; for he is coming, for he is coming to judge the earth. He will judge the world with righteousness . . . and truth" (Ps 96: 10–13). Elsewhere the Psalmist writes, "Let the nations be glad and sing for joy, for you [God] judge the peoples with equity and guide the nations upon earth" (Ps 67:4). The reason for such joy in the face of judgement is because in the last judgement God will disclose his righteousness and truth, and will put an end to all deception, seduction, illusion, and ambiguity. God will publicly and definitively vindicate the oppressed.

Psalm 98 declares, "He [God] has revealed his vindication in the sight of the nations. . . . Make a joyful noise to the LORD, all the earth; break forth into joyous song, . . . for he is coming to judge the earth. He will judge the world with righteousness, and the people with equity" (Ps 98:2, 4, 9). God publicly reveals himself as universal King of all creation, one whose role includes defending the wronged, and putting things right. Stephen Travis comments, "The emphasis on restorative justice is not on 'paying back' the offender, but on positively 'putting right what has gone wrong

---

117. Thiselton, *Doubt, Faith and Certainty*, 10–11 and 61–75.
118. Thiselton, *Doubt, Faith and Certainty*, 61–64.
119. Martin Luther, cited in Rupp and Drewery, *Martin Luther*, 20.

between the offender and the victim."[120] In Isa 45:21–22, God is called "A righteous God and a Savior." God's final, definitive, and unrevisable verdict will constitute a final "putting right" of all, which justification by faith anticipates.[121] The last judgement is what philosophers of speech-act theory would call performative speech act, a transformative act of God. It will be the performative speech act of judgement, which will constitute a transformative verdict involving genuine action.[122] This is entirely in accord with Paul's note of confidence, especially his confidence in God.

Questions for reflection

1. Are we too often misled by the "spatial" contrast between the seen or material world and the realm of "beyond"? How much would it help if we were more in line with the Bible's *temporal* contrast between "now" and God's future?

2. How much would it help us if we distinguished more clearly between "external" evaluations or viewpoints, and how God sees our "inward self"? Do we too often focus on "externals"? Can we, like Elisha or A. G. Hogg see beyond the present world?

3. What role does the resurrection of the spiritual "body" have in encouraging our faith and life? Or are we simply mesmerized by the experience of "wasting away," as if this were the only thing that matters? What about the "house not made with hands," i.e., a building made by God?

4. How much is belief in the resurrection governed by our belief in God as sovereign Creator?

5. Is the concept of an "intermediate state" actually dissolved by distinguishing between an "observer" and "participant" viewpoint?

6. Do we expect a genuine transformation in the resurrection or simply a continued life after death?

---

120. Travis, *Christ and the Judgement of God*, 8.
121. Cf. Yinger, *Paul, Judaism, and judgement according to Deeds*, 284–90.
122. On this speech-act philosophy cf. Austin, *How to Do Things with Words*, 88–91, 152–56, 162; Donald Evans, *The Logic of Self-Involvement*, 36 and throughout; Searle, *Expression and Meaning*; and Thiselton, *Thiselton on Hermeneutics*, 51–150.

7. Does it help to think of this life as a pilgrimage to prepare us for the next?
8. Do we too readily limit what the Holy Spirit will do by what he does now?
9. What does Paul mean by "faith" when he sets it in contrast to sight?
10. Why do Old Testament believers look forward to the last judgment with keen anticipation and joy? What is it about the judgment that makes us look forward to it without anxiety?

6. The ministry of reconciliation (5:11—6:2)

(a) Paul's ministry (5:11–17)

[11] Therefore, knowing the fear of the Lord, we try to persuade others; but we ourselves are well known to God, and I hope that we are also well known to your consciences. [12] We are not commending ourselves to you again, but giving you an opportunity to boast about us, so that you may be able to answer those who boast in outward appearance and not in the heart. [13] For if we are beside ourselves, it is for God; if we are in our right mind, it is for you. [14] For the love of Christ urges us on, because we are convinced that one has died for all; therefore all have died. [15] And he died for all, so that those who live might live no longer for themselves, but for him who died and was raised for them.

[16] From now on, therefore, we regard no one from a human point of view; even though we once knew Christ from a human point of view, we know him no longer in that way. [17] So if anyone is in Christ, there is a new creation: everything old has passed away; see, everything has become new!

The first section of this passage speaks of the treasure of the gospel ambassador's message and the new creation that arises from Christ's death (5:11–21). In v. 11, Paul reaffirms that the minister's or apostle's task is to *persuade*. He still has in mind the contrast between the treasure of the gospel message and the earthenware jars that contain it. Apostles or ministers may be commissioned to persuade, but they are fragile and vulnerable vehicles. They still stand under the judgment of God or "fear of the Lord." Paul's reference to "consciences" reflects the accusation by some that Paul's preaching is manipulative. Again, Paul insists on his sincerity and his reverential awareness that God sees all.

The next verse (5:12) continues the thought: Paul is not commending himself, in contrast to his opponents in Corinth. His ministry is "open," in contrast also to Moses use of the veil in Exod 34. Complete openness can be a source of the right kind of "boasting," boasting authentic apostleship. Paul tells us that he has spoken in "tongues" (1 Cor 14:18) and will say the he has been "exalted to the third heaven" (2 Cor 12:2–3). It is not out of character that he tells us that "We can be beside ourselves" (Greek, *eite exestēmen*; second aorist active indicative of *existēmi*, to stand out of oneself, from *ekstasis*, ecstasy).

"We" (v. 13) is a literary plural, i.e., it refers to Paul himself. He wants the Corinthians to know the facts. "Outward appearance" refers to the false boasts of the opponents of Paul who make a different kind of boast. A. T. Robertson calls them the "braggarts."[123] The aorist may point to specific occasions in the past. "We are in our right mind" is to indicate that rational, reasonable, or non-ecstatic discourse functions to give pastoral ministry for the benefit of the readers.

Paul goes on to point out that his ministry is compelled (Greek, *synechei hēmas*, literally *to press hard* or *to hold together*; NRSV, *urges us on*; NIV, *to compel*, RSV, *to control*, v. 14) by the love (Greek, *hē agapē*) of Christ.[124] "Of Christ" is subjective genitive, i.e., Christ's love for Paul and others. Christ's love has taken hold of Paul. He then elaborates in what Christ's love consists. He has already made a judgment (Greek, *krinantas touto*, i.e., *"because we have concluded"*) that "one has died for all." In Thrall's words, "It is Christ's love for humanity that exercises its influence upon Paul."[125] His belief in the effective love of Christ goes on to affirm what is common to early Christianity. He may therefore be appealing to common conviction. The phrase "He died for all" (v. 15) is the common apostolic faith of the church. The Greek preposition *hyper* (for) is crucial here: it can mean "on behalf of" or "for the benefit of." The New Testament also uses more explicitly substitutionary prepositions (Greek, *anti*, instead of, as in Mark 10:45; Matt 17:27; cf. Rom 12:17; 1 Cor 11:15; 1 Thess 5:15). But A. T. Robertson suggests that *hyper* is used here "in the sense of substitution" also, as in John 11:50, and is more usual than *anti*.[126]

---

123. Robertson, *Word Pictures in the NT*, vol. 4, 230.
124. Danker, BDAG, 970–71 includes all these meanings for *synechō*.
125. Thrall, *Second Corinthians*, 408.
126. Robertson, *Word Pictures in the NT*, vol. 4, 230–31; cf. Thrall, *Second Corinthians*, 409.

"Therefore all died" does not exclude substitution but includes participation alongside it. Thrall discusses six possible interpretations of this clause. She includes as the most convincing the presupposition of Christ-union and its effects, as in Rom 6:3-4. We must take account, she says, of what Paul says elsewhere about participation and being in Christ. Substitution and participation are "a 'both-and' rather than 'either-or.'"[127] In v. 5, she continues, "Paul indicates now that its purpose was "to bring to an end man's self-centred existence," which is the essence of the fallen state.[128] Those who "live for themselves" might constitute a secondary allusion to the false apostles at Corinth.

A second section begins at vv. 16-17. Paul regards no one "from a human point of view" (Greek, *kata sarka*). He does not regard even Christ in this way. The reference to Christ clarifies what he means by the Greek *sarx*. To know Christ in this way would be to know him on the basis of his "external" characteristics or natural attributes: as a figure born on a certain date, son of Mary and Joseph, raised in a given cultural environment, and leader of twelve disciples. But neither Jesus nor others can be evaluated by purely human criteria or worldly standards. Paul admits that once he knew Christ in this kind of way. But in the next verse (v. 17) he will say that everything has become new in the new creation: "In Christ there is a new creation." Paul was not a believer when he knew Jesus only in term of class, race, and cultural background. The new creation becomes a dividing point between two different kinds of knowledge. Guthrie comments, "Evaluation of Christ himself on worldly terms may be seen as the permanent absurdity, for Paul had been confronted by Christ the Lord on the road to Damascus, and all his misjudgments lay shattered in the dust."[129]

In v. 17, Paul uses the phrase "in Christ," which occurs seventy-six times in Paul. He uses the term "in Christ" in a variety of contexts with different meanings, as Johannes Weiss points out. (i) "In Christ" may sometimes be used to mean "because Christ has come." (ii) It may be used in a representative sense, as in 1 Cor 15:22, "as in Adam all die, in Christ shall all be made alive." (iii) Sometimes it is a simple preposition: "to boast in Christ (1 Cor 1:31). (iv) Weiss also includes an instrumental use (1 Thess 4:1). (v) It includes a mystical sense, as in Phil 4:1, "I can do all things through Christ." Yet the most theologically important and characteristic

---

127. Thrall, *Second Corinthians*, 411.
128. Thrall, *Second Corinthians*, 411.
129. Guthrie, *2 Corinthians*, 307.

THE AUTHENTIC MINISTRY DESCRIBED AND DEFENDED

sense is illustrated in "There is no condemnation to those who are in Christ Jesus," where Paul refers to being "bound-up-in-a-bundle with Christ in such a way that God sees them as part of Christ."[130] Weiss calls this the eschatological status of Christ-union, and Bultmann argues the same point.[131] Our one reservation about Bultmann, however, is that he uses Paul's disparagement of "fleshly" knowledge of Jesus to devalue historical enquiry about Jesus. But, as W. D. Davies comments, "What he [Paul] is repudiating is not a fleshly kind of Christ but a fleshly kind of knowledge."[132] Thrall considers that "in Christ" may mean "the personal unity of the believer with Christ," but adds that corporate personality lies in the background, so the phrase may also mean to have become incorporated into the community that is the body of Christ.[133]

Questions for reflection

1. Why does God choose to mediate the treasure of the gospel in frail earthenware jars? What does this tell us about ordained ministers and ourselves?

2. In 2 Corinthians, Paul states that the task of ambassadors is to persuade. But how does his reference to "consciences" modify or qualify this?

3. Paul does not disparage exceptional "spiritual" experiences of God or Christ. Yet how does he limit these experiences? For what purpose does he commend reasonable, logical, or normal, discourse?

4. Christ's love for the world has taken hold of Paul. How does he immediately respond and react?

5. What is the basis or criterion for evaluating both Jesus Christ and other people? Is this a matter of birth, culture, and education, or is there something more? Does being a "new creation" make a difference to us?

6. In how many ways can we understand "in Christ"? What is the most important and characteristically Pauline use?

---

130. Weiss, *History of Primitive Christianity*, vol. 2, 468–69.
131. Bultmann *Second Corinthians*, 157.
132. Davies, *Paul and Rabbinic Judaism*, 195.
133. Thrall, *Second Corinthians*, 425.

(b) A ministry of reconciliation (5:18—6:2)

¹⁸ All this is from God, who reconciled us to himself through Christ, and has given us the ministry of reconciliation; ¹⁹ that is, in Christ God was reconciling the world to himself, not counting their trespasses against them, and entrusting the message of reconciliation to us. ²⁰ So we are ambassadors for Christ, since God is making his appeal through us; we entreat you on behalf of Christ, be reconciled to God. ²¹ For our sake he made him to be sin who knew no sin, so that in him we might become the righteousness of God.

6 As we work together with him, we urge you also not to accept the grace of God in vain. ² For he says, "At an acceptable time I have listened to you, and on a day of salvation I have helped you." See, now is the acceptable time; see, now is the day of salvation!

Guthrie begins a new section with vv. 18–19, which he entitles "God's program of reconciliation and Paul's mission."[134] The new creation comes "from God," and he has given two things: first, he has reconciled us to himself; second, he has given to us the ministry of reconciliation. "Us" is again a literary plural standing for Paul. The world is the scope of reconciliation. "Reconciliation" (Greek, *katallagē*; verb, *katallassō*) is a word distinctive to Paul. It was part of Paul's genius to introduce the term "reconciliation" to denote the reversal of sinners' situation of alienation from God, or even to reverse hostility toward him. The Greek noun *katallagē* includes "reestablishment of an interrupted or broken relationship," while the verb *katallassō* denotes "the exchange of hostility for a friendly relationship" or "to reconcile."[135]

It once might have been difficult to expound what used to look like a theological term, but nowadays we are all familiar with reconciliation between separated husbands and wives, and between potentially warring nations, and between employers and trades unions. Paul uses the term in Rom 5:10-11 and 1 Cor 7:11 of reconciliation between husband and wife. In 2 Cor 5:18-19, Paul states that God has reconciled us to himself through Christ and calls the gospel "the ministry of reconciliation." This naturally leads on to v. 20, "Be reconciled to God." In the shorter epistles Paul writes, "God was pleased to reconcile to himself all things," even though the readers were once "estranged and hostile in mind" (Col 1:20-22).

---

134. Guthrie, *2 Corinthians*, 308.
135. Danker, BDAG, 521.

James Denney insists that reconciliation "is a work which is finished, . . . a work outside of us, in which God so deals in Christ with the sin of the world that it shall no longer be a barrier between himself and man."[136] Denney is right to emphasize this "objective or finished" side, but reconciliation also includes the human side in which the Holy Spirit makes real or "actualizes" the new relationship of welcome in our everyday lives. Hence, Paul adds, "We entreat you on behalf of Christ, be reconciled to God" (2 Cor 5:20).[137] The Greek for "we are ambassadors" (*presbeuomen*) Danker renders "work as an ambassador," as in Eph 6:20.[138] Adolf Deissmann provides examples from the papyri of its use for being the Emperor's legate.[139] Paul therefore has a natural pride in the status and office. As Robertson comments, the Legate had to be accepted in both countries: the one he represents and the one to which he has been sent. God speaks through Paul as Christ's Legate.[140]

Many writers regard v. 21 as a clear sign of substitutionary sacrifice, since Paul clearly states that Jesus was without sin, yet God "made him to be sin" (Greek, *hamartian epoiēsen*). Thrall sees this as an expansion of v. 19a, explaining how "the 'non-reckoning' of sins was made possible and relates the motif of reconciliation to that of justification."[141] But in what sense was Christ "made to be sin"? Thrall traces two main interpretations in the church fathers: *sin* may mean *sin-offering* (probably the majority view in the West); or it may refer to "suffering the fate of sinners." In modern times, Whiteley is one of the most robust defenders of the second view. He renders the phrase "God made him [Christ] one with the sinfulness on men."[142] At the other end of the spectrum, Leon Morris boldly attacks Whiteley's view head-on. He writes, "All the verbal juggling in the world cannot make 'made sin' mean 'took upon himself human nature' which is [in effect] Whiteley's interpretation."[143]

Furnish provides a more moderate version of Whiteley's view by rejecting "sin offering" (as in Lev 4:25, 29) on the ground that it does not fit

---

136. Denney, *The Death of Christ*, 145.
137. Cf. Thiselton, *Systematic Theology*, 201-3.
138. Danker, BDAG, 861.
139. Deissmann, *Light from the Ancient East*, 374.
140. Robertson, *Word Pictures*, vol. 4, 233.
141. Thrall, *Second Corinthians*, 439.
142. Whiteley, *The Theology of St. Paul*, 136.
143. Morris, *The Cross in the New Testament*, 332-33.

the context, although he also recognized that it may reflect the background of Isa 53:6, 9: "The LORD has laid on him the iniquity of us all."[144] Bultmann broadly agrees with Furnish. But once we engage with the context it is also hard to see that the incarnation would provide a Pauline context of thought rather than a direct reference to the death of Christ. Guthrie traces the flow of Paul's thought with care, and concludes, "The significance . . . for the present verse has to do with Christ being a fit, 'unblemished' substitutionary sacrifice for sins," as Bruce and Martin convincingly argue.[145] Martin and Barrett regard Gal 3:13 as similar.[146] Barrett argues, "Paul develops the thought in terms of exchange: Christ was made *sin*, that we might become *God's righteousness*. . . . Christ became sin; that is, he came to stand in that relation with God which normally is the result of sin, estranged from God and the object of his wrath."[147] "Christ redeemed us from the curse of the law when he became a curse."[148] Gregory of Nazianzus similarly regards Christ as making humanity's disobedience his own, as though he was a sinner, calling him (Greek) *autoamartia*.

Paul continues this thought in 6:1–2. As ever, the key ground of appeal is God's grace. Guthrie calls this short section "The applied conclusion to Paul's theological reflections on reconciliation begun at 5:18."[149] "We work together with him" (v. 1) shows that we are partners or co-workers with God, as in 1 Cor 3:9. (Paul seems here to use "we" in a wider sense to include all believers.) The Greek *charis* (grace) is "probably comprehensive, including all the various aspects of the grace of salvation and especially the blessings of justification and reconciliation."[150] The Corinthians are not to receive it "in vain" (Greek, *kenos*), i.e., not to let it amount to nothing. For God says, "In an acceptable time (Greek, *kairō dektō . . . kairos euprosdektos*) I have listened to you." The comment is a quotation from Isa 49:8. The double compound *en + pros + dektos*, derives from the Greek verb *dechomai*, which means "well received."

The Greek word *kairos* means a favorable moment or the right time, in contrast to the Greek *chronos*, which means a period or length of time,

---

144. Furnish, *II Corinthians*, 341 and 351.
145. Guthrie, *2 Corinthians*, 313.
146. Martin, *2 Corinthians*, 157.
147. Barrett, *Second Corinthians*, 180 (his italics).
148. Barrett, *Second Corinthians*, 180.
149. Guthrie, *2 Corinthians*, 315.
150. Thrall, *Second Corinthians* 451.

as Cullmann and others pointed out long ago.[151] God often appoints a "favorable moment" for his work of grace. Sometimes, as in Hebrews, this is called "Today." This moment can be lost if we delay inordinately. Paul calls the acceptable time "the day of salvation" (6:2). Isaiah's words demand a response. A prayer by Kate McIlhagga expresses the point: "God of all time, God beyond and behind time, may we know when it is too late and what is too soon. May we always recognize the right time in the light of your timeless love."[152]

Questions for reflection

1. In what ways does the use of the word "reconciliation" mark a special achievement of Paul? In what contexts does its use in modern life provide a bridge to its meaning in the New Testament?
2. In what sense can James Denney insist that reconciliation is "done" or "finished," and in what sense is this first comment incomplete?
3. What does it mean to be an "ambassador"? When should ambassadors be received and welcomed?
4. In what sense did God make Christ "sin"? Does this imply that he died as a substitute for us? What else might it imply?
5. Is it possible to receive God's grace in vain? What would this mean?
6. How does the word "favorable moment" (Greek, *kairos*) challenge us? Can it also encourage us?

7. The apostolic credentials of Paul's mission (6:3–10)

> ³ We are putting no obstacle in anyone's way, so that no fault may be found with our ministry, ⁴ but as servants of God we have commended ourselves in every way: through great endurance, in afflictions, hardships, calamities, ⁵ beatings, imprisonments, riots, labors, sleepless nights, hunger; ⁶ by purity, knowledge, patience, kindness, holiness of spirit, genuine love, ⁷ truthful speech, and the power of God; with the weapons of righteousness for the right hand and for the left; ⁸ in honor and dishonor, in ill repute and good repute. We are treated as impostors, and yet are true; ⁹ as

---

151. Cullmann, *Christ and Time*, 39–44; Danker, BDAG, 497–98.
152. Quoted in Angela Ashwin, *The Book of a Thousand Prayers*, 111.

unknown, and yet are well known; as dying, and see—we are alive; as punished, and yet not killed; [10] as sorrowful, yet always rejoicing; as poor, yet making many rich; as having nothing, and yet possessing everything.

In v. 3, most of the words are significant. NRSV's "no fault may be found with our ministry" renders the Greek *mē mōmēthē hē diakonia*. The Greek verb *mōmaomai* does mean find fault with or blame; but Hughes and Plummer argue that the word also "conveys the suggestion of mocking and ridicule."[153] It is a rare word, used again in 2 Cor 8:20, and in Prov 9:7 (LXX). Hughes quotes Calvin as saying, "It is an artifice of Satan to seek some misconduct on the part of ministers which may tend to the dishonour of the gospel; for when he has been successful in bringing the ministry into contempt, all hope of progress is destroyed."[154] It would be ridiculous to strive to maintain a reputation before others while inviting reproach by a shameful life. Further, the rhetorical compiling of negatives in alliterative form is striking: in Greek *mēdemian + mēdeni + mē*. Finally, Paul uses the late word *proskopēn* for *obstacle* or *cause of stumbling*, which Danker renders "an occasion for taking offence"; he adds "Christians are not to provide outsiders with any reason for finding fault with the Christian message."[155] Paul more often uses the Greek *proskomma, an offence,* (Rom 14:20; 1 Cor 8:9).

In v. 4, Paul resumes the tricky question of self-commendation. He actually says, "As servants of God we commend ourselves in every way," when earlier he seems to have renounced letters of commendation. But the list of hardships in vv. 4b–5 states how different is Paul's self-commendation from the commendations sought by the false apostles. These "false apostles" would not for one moment consider listing "endurance, afflictions, hardships, calamities" (Greek, *en thlipsin, en anagkais, en stenochōriais*) (v. 4b), let alone "in beatings" (Greek, *en plēgais*), "in imprisonments" (*en phylakais*), . . . "in hunger," and other afflictions in v. 5. *Stenochōriais* could refer to stressful situations. "Beatings" includes blows and wounds inflicted probably by whips or ropes. Each word carries a picture of the narrative of Paul's life as a pastor and preacher. A comparable "catalogue of hardships" occurs in 2 Cor 11:23–27, and we earlier referred to a similar list, in 1 Cor 4:8–13; 15:30–31; and 2 Cor 1:8–10; 2:4; 4:17; with much specialist literature, including such

---

153. Danker, BDAG, 663; Hughes, *Second Corinthians*, 221; cf. Plummer, *Second Corinthians*, 192.

154. Hughes, *Second Corinthians*, 221.

155. Danker, BDAG, 882.

"lists" by J. T. Fitzgerald, Karl Plank, S. J. Hafemann, and others. In v. 5, Paul includes sleepless nights, riots (Greek, *en akatastasiais*) and other hardships that imply repeated horrors.

Guthrie writes about vv. 6–7a, "If the first ten phrases in Paul's description present a picture of the challenges surrounding authentic ministry, the next eight delineate the first manner in which Paul's mission has been carried out (6:6 a) and then the means (6:6b) by which his ministry has been enabled."[156] In purity, in knowledge, in patience, and in kindness, denote the *manner*; in the Holy Spirit, in genuine love, in the word of truth, and in the power of God, denote the *means*. The Greek *hagnotēs* may denote purity of behavior or sincerity of motive. In 11:3, the word functions as the opposite of corruption. Three of the terms (Greek, *makrothymia* (patience), *agapē* (love), and *chrēstotēs* (kindness) appear in Gal 5:22 as the fruit of the Holy Spirit.[157] Paul insists on the purity of his intentions. "Knowledge" (*gnosis*) is generally used unfavorably in Paul, e.g., in 1 Cor 8:1. Thrall therefore argues that it refers to "charismatic gnosis." But in 1 Corinthians it refers to a claim to *complete* or *static* knowledge, whereas Paul approves of growing or *dynamic* knowledge as a process, in which the Holy Spirit is active. "Truthful speech" (v. 4a) is repeated in this letter (cf. 4:2). In v. 7b, "weapons of righteousness for the right hand and for the left" may well mean offensive and defensive weapons, for the sword was carried in the right hand, and a shield in the left. "Righteousness" may well refer to human moral righteousness in contrast to manipulative tactics.

We may infer that some in Corinth thought that Paul had tried to deceive them. Jesus had suffered the same accusation (Matt. 27:63). The apostle denies this, insisting that his speech is truthful and honest. In v. 9, he insists the apostles are "as unknown, yet well known," by which he means unrecognized in the public world of learning and politics, and not sought after like famous rhetoricians, but well known among the churches, especially the Pauline communities.[158] Barrett also renders this "unrecognized . . . as an apostle" yet "recognized" certainly by God but also by the so-called Pillars in Jerusalem (Gal 1:12, 16). Robertson suggests "ignored as nonentities, obscure, without proper credentials." These "paradoxes" make good sense against the background of 2 Cor 10–13.

---

156. Guthrie, *2 Corinthians*, 329.
157. Thrall, *Second Corinthians*, 459.
158. Thrall, *Second Corinthians*, 464–65; Guthrie, *2 Corinthians*, 335.

The "paradox" "as dying and see—we are alive" (v. 9) reflects the reality of 11:19. In v. 10, the fifth contrast, "as sorrowful, yet always rejoicing" (Greek, *hōs lypoumenoi aei de chairontes*) reflects the reality of not only 11:19; but also 1 Thess 5:16; Rom 5:3–5; 9:2. It describes the life of the authentic apostle as Paul found this in everyday life. The sixth contrast, "as poor yet making many rich" describes the apostles' literal lack of reliable financial income, side by side with their abundance of spiritual resources and the effects of their ministry (cf. 11:7–10). The "paradoxical" character of Christian ministry is constantly underlined in this epistle.

The "false" apostles in Corinth may have anticipated the so-called "prosperity gospel" in viewing financial success as a sign of God's blessing and approval. Furnish rightly regards Paul's impoverishment as a "failure" in the eyes of the Corinthians, and a tacit admission that he lacks apostolic authority (cf. 1 Cor 9:1–18; 2 Cor 11:7–11).[159] They assumed that Paul's admission—"having nothing"—made their case. But because they belong to Christ, *everything* belongs to them (cf. 1 Cor 3:21–22). There is a play on words in the Greek: the Greek word *echo* simply means *to have*; the compound word *katechō* means *to hold fast* or *to possess* (v. 10).

Questions for reflection

1. How many pastors and clergy suffer mocking and ridicule for something that is deemed distasteful by "outsiders"? Do we give them needed support? Or on the contrary, how many pastors and clergy ruin their reputation by some blatant discrepancy in their everyday lives?
2. Do we associate Paul's "catalogue of hardships" with genuine Christian vocation, or do we view hardships as a sign of failure or disobedience? On the other hand, does the catalogue of hardships apply to apostles only?
3. How often does Paul list samples of his "hardships"?
4. How often do "patience" and "kindness" save a fraught situation? How do "hardships" which we may have suffered as Christians compare with Paul's?

---

159. Furnish, *II Corinthians*, 359.

5. Does it weigh with us if we are "nonentities" in the world of politics and learning as long as we are "recognized" in our churches or among Christians?
6. Can we still rejoice even when finances are precarious? Is this a sign that God has abandoned us?

8. A plea for openness and purity: the temple of the Living God (6:11—7:4)

(a) Openness and purity (6:11–18)

¹¹ We have spoken frankly to you Corinthians; our heart is wide open to you. ¹² There is no restriction in our affections, but only in yours. ¹³ In return—I speak as to children—open wide your hearts also.

¹⁴ Do not be mismatched with unbelievers. For what partnership is there between righteousness and lawlessness? Or what fellowship is there between light and darkness? ¹⁵ What agreement does Christ have with Beliar? Or what does a believer share with an unbeliever? ¹⁶ What agreement has the temple of God with idols? For we are the temple of the living God; as God said,

"I will live in them and walk among them,
 and I will be their God,
 and they shall be my people.
¹⁷ Therefore come out from them,
 and be separate from them, says the Lord,
 and touch nothing unclean;
 then I will welcome you,
¹⁸ and I will be your father,
 and you shall be my sons and daughters,
 says the Lord Almighty."

Paul expresses his warm affection for the church in Corinth in 6:11–13. He has opened his heart to them as well as speaking frankly. He tells them that he has kept back nothing; there has been no restraint whatever on his side, and he says that if there has been any restraint it must have been in their hearts. His phrase "our heart is wide" renders the Greek *hē kardia hēmōn peplatuntai*, the perfect passive indicative of *platunō*, to broaden from *platus*, broad. The vocative "Corinthians" is unusual in Paul but may serve to include the whole Corinthian church. Whether Paul is referring

PART II: EXEGESIS

to what he has said so far in 2 Corinthians or includes his earlier utterances is debated. His "catalogue of hardships" may suggest that his frankness about the supposedly negative side of his ministry could have gone further than he had intended.

The Greek *stenochōreō* (restriction, v. 12) implies to confine to a narrow space, or to cramp emotionally.[160] By contrast, the Greek *splanchnon* metaphorically depicts strong affection, intimate love, and emotion. Paul pleads for reciprocal openness on the readers' part. The Greek word *antimisthian* (in return, v. 13) is used to denote a reciprocal transaction or an appropriate recompense. Given Paul's lavish expenditure of time and affection on the readers, would it be too much to hope for the same understanding from them? His second plea is to the readers as "children." This entirely reflects 1 Cor 4:15, where Paul tells the church in Corinth that they may have ten thousand instructors, but only one spiritual "father." This term is not used to impose authority in an authoritarian way, contrary to what Castelli urges.[161] "Father" expresses intimacy and affection rather than authority here.

From 6:14 to 7:1, Paul renews his plea for purity. Hence the beginning of this section, "Do not be mismatched with unbelievers," is not such an abrupt change of topic as some maintain, even suggesting that it comes from another letter. Guthrie comments, "There are good arguments against this perspective: the passage may be read as integrative with the surrounding material."[162] Hafemann, Beale, Thrall, and David Hall agree with Guthrie's approach.[163] Hall considers Paul's language, internal consistency, and psychological arguments. Paul reinforces and even restates earlier exhortations that call the Corinthians to separate from inappropriate worldly relations. The mention of idols in the last of the rhetorical questions gives rise to "We are the temple of the living God." Intimacy with God demands separation from what is unclean.

In v. 14, the word translated "mismatched" (Greek, *heterozygountes*, literally *yoked with what is other*) is without parallel in the New Testament. The present imperative suggests "Stop becoming yoked," in contrast to the

---

160. Danker, BDAG, 942.

161. Castelli, *Imitating Paul*, 97–115.

162. Guthrie, *2 Corinthians*, 346.

163. Beale, "The Old Testament Background of Reconciliation in 2 Corinthians 5–7 and Its Bearing on the Literary Problem of 2 Corinthians 6:14–71"; Hafemann, *2 Corinthians*, 277; and Hall, *The Unity of the Corinthian Correspondence*, 87–100 and 113–14.

aorist subjunctive, i.e., some are already guilty of this.[164] The prohibition of "mixtures" comes from Lev 19:19, and more broadly Deut 22: 9ff. Deuteronomy forbids plowing with a calf and a donkey. As Barrett comments, this was expanded in the Mishnah.[165] Spicq confirms the metaphorical use of Greek, *heterozygeō* to include a wider application.[166]

It is well known that among the Exclusive Brethren this verse is used not only of marriage to unbelievers, but is also applied to business partnerships and other areas. This might not have been unreasonable in Paul's day, for business partnerships then involved participation in possible pagan cults. One writer renders it "Stop being in incompatible relationships," leaving unspecified which relationships are included. Plummer simply suggests that this is not confined to mixed marriages.[167] Hence, the translation "Be not mismated" seems too restrictive. Paul certainly states several sets of incompatible relations, e.g., righteousness and lawlessness, light and darkness, Christ and Beliar, believer and unbeliever (v. 15). It has been suggested that Paul incorporates part of a sermon that he had composed earlier. The climax comes in v. 16, "the temple of the living God and idols": how can there be any agreement (Greek, *synkatathesis*) between them?

Paul then quotes Lev 26:11–12; Isa 52:11; Ezek 20:34; 37:27; and 2 Sam 7:8, 14. In these passages, the theme is: "I will be their God and they my people"; this is the ground of the command "Come out and be separate." If God is holy, his people must be holy too.[168] "Beliar" only occurs here. It is a proper name more commonly rendered "Belial," used in Jewish writings for Satan. Thrall suggests that Paul uses an unfamiliar term for rhetorical effect. "Harmony" (Greek, *symphōnēsis*) could simply mean "agreement."[169] He also implies that a believer and unbeliever have nothing genuinely in common, even if his concessions about pre-existing mixed marriages in 1 Cor 7:12–15 may modify this thought. His fifth and last rhetorical question shows that there can be no compromise with idolatry. This may look back to his discussion in 1 Cor 8 and 10. In 1 Cor 10:21, Paul had said, "You cannot drink the cup of the Lord and the cup of demons." In v. 16, he refers to the Christian community as God's temple, as he did

---

164. Robertson, *Word Pictures*, vol. 4, 236.
165. Barrett, *Second Corinthians*, 195.
166. Spicq, *Theological Lexicon of the New Testament*, vol. 2, 80–81.
167. Plummer, *Second Corinthians*, 206.
168. Cf. Thrall, *Second Corinthians*, 471–74.
169. Barrett, *Second Corinthians*, 197–98.

already in 1 Cor 3:16–17 ("For we are the temple of the living God"), and in more individual terms in 1 Cor 6:19, where the body of the Christian is the temple of the Holy Spirit. For a formerly conservative Jew, this revaluation of the temple is impressive.

In v. 17, Paul repeats the Old Testament command, "Come out from them and be separate from them, says the Lord." The corollary is that God will welcome them and be their Father (vv. 17–18). They must be separate from the pollution of the pagan world. The first quotation comes from Isa 52:11 (referring to Babylon); the second from Ezek 20:34. Christians can find a parallel with God's restoration of Israel in its history. This passage confirms the familial relationship of Christians to God. The concept of believers as sons is found in Rom 8:14–17 and Gal 3:26; 4:6–7. The addition "and daughters" (v. 18) occurs only here in Paul. Barrett and Martin regard this as a deliberate addition of Paul to an Old Testament quotation.[170] The Greek term *pantokratōr* means "almighty," and Peter Geach and Gjisbert Van der Brink infinitely prefer this biblical term to the Latin-derived "omnipotent." They argue that it avoids some supposed contradictions in philosophy from which the biblical, Greek, term is exempt, while indicate God's absolute sovereignty.

Questions for reflection

1. Does deep affection imply that speech can be frank and bold? Is any limit or qualification suggested? Are we ever too frank or less than frank about our "hardships"?
2. What kind of "mismatch" with unbelievers can most threaten us? Where do we draw the line between Christian values and secular culture?
3. Do we too easily dismiss passages about purity in Leviticus and Deuteronomy as referring only to Israel? Why does Paul cite a string of Old Testament passages to a mainly gentile congregation?

---

170. Barrett, *Second Corinthians*, 201; Martin, *2 Corinthians*, 206–7.

THE AUTHENTIC MINISTRY DESCRIBED AND DEFENDED

(b) Paul's repeated appeal (7:1–4)

> Since we have these promises, beloved, let us cleanse ourselves from every defilement of body and of spirit, making holiness perfect in the fear of God.
> ² Make room in your hearts for us; we have wronged no one, we have corrupted no one, we have taken advantage of no one. ³ I do not say this to condemn you, for I said before that you are in our hearts, to die together and to live together. ⁴ I often boast about you; I have great pride in you; I am filled with consolation; I am overjoyed in all our affliction.

Paul now concludes his argument in 7:1. The word "promises" (Greek, *epangeliai*) is doubtless used, as Martin suggests, because the words from Scripture (6:16–18) are messianic.[171] This may equally denote covenant promises. In either case, the word "these" is emphatic here. The string of Old Testament passages certainly incudes the promise of 2 Sam 7:8–17 ("I will raise up your offspring . . . and I will establish his kingdom," v. 12), spoken by Nathan of the Davidic heir. The promises constitute the basis on which the Corinthians are exhorted to respond. Longing for God as Father is primary. The Corinthians are "beloved" not because of their conduct but because they are God's beloved covenant people. Because they belong to God Paul exhorts them to avoid immorality and impurity. The Greek term *molysmos* denotes defilement in both a religious and moral sense and occurs in the LXX. The Maccabees used the term of threatened Hellenization and pagan compromise. Holiness is to be made "perfect" (NRSV) or "completed" (Greek, *epiteleō*) in proper reverence for God, to whom we belong as a people.

7:2–4 clinches the argument. Paul again appeals for affection, but is still troubled about whether the Corinthians still suspect his motives or conduct. In view of this nagging concern, the supposedly abrupt change of tone in chapters 10–13 is not entirely surprising, as Martin implies.[172] Guthrie comments, "Perhaps the harshness of Paul's past rebukes (2:1–3; 7:8) had been construed as abuse by some."[173] Paul says that this is unjust. He insists, "We have wronged no one (Greek, *oudena edikēsamen*), we have corrupted no one (Greek, *oudena ephtheiramen*), we have taken advantage of no one" (Greek, *oudena epleonektēsamen*, v. 2). Plummer observes that these words may refer

---

171. Martin, *2 Corinthians*, 207.
172. Martin, *2 Corinthians*, 218.
173. Guthrie, *2 Corinthians*, 362.

to money, or morals, or doctrine.[174] Thrall suggests that moral corruption may have been wrongly inferred from Paul's teaching about freedom from the law, but whatever the case about that, some certainly seem to have been attacking his moral probity. That charge was made in Thessalonica (1 Thess 4:6). Paul therefore pleads with them that their love should not have cooled: "Make room in your hearts" (Greek, *chōrēsate hēmas*). Thrall observes that the whole theme concerns the heart (v. 3).[175] Both life and death are aspects of genuine ministry. In Rom 8:38–39, Paul says that neither life nor death can separate us from the love of God.

In spite of the attack on Paul by the "false apostles," he can still affirm not only his genuine affection for the Corinthians, but also his genuine confidence and pride or "boast" (Greek, *kauchēsis*) in them (v. 4). Paul is proud to tell others that the Corinthians are one of "his" own people.[176] Denney and Barrett translate "confidence" (Greek, *parresia*) as boldness or freedom of speech, and Guthrie as boldness or openness.[177] Paul ends this section with a note of encouragement.

Questions for reflection

1. What are today's "idols"? Do consumerism, immorality, and apostasy from God feature in our thinking as we evaluate secular culture? How can we best protect our children from such influences?

2. Can we say with Paul that we have wronged no one, and taken advantage of no one? Plummer applies these words to money, morals, and Christian teaching.

3. Can we still be proud or confident of fellow-Christians even when a particular Christian group has misunderstood and criticized us?

---

174. Plummer, *Second Corinthians*, 213.

175. Thrall, *Second Corinthians*, 483.

176. Martin, *2 Corinthians*, 221.

177. Denney, *2 Corinthians*, 248; Barrett, *Second Corinthians*, 193; Guthrie, *2 Corinthians*, 363.

IV

THE ARRIVAL OF TITUS IN MACEDONIA

7:5–16

After Paul's main concern about authentic ministry in 2:14—7:4, Titus safely arrives back in Macedonia, and Paul resumes his travel narrative, which he recounted in 2:12-13 and 7:5-6. In 2:13, he says that he had found no rest because he had not yet found Titus. He recalls this experience in 7:5. 2 Corinthians 7:5-16 focuses, first, on the encouraging report that he received concerning the Corinthians, especially that they had received his harsh letter well (7:6-7); second, Paul reflects further on the positive effects of his letter (7:8-13a); third, he tells of Titus' joy at the Corinthians' response (7:13b-16).[1]

1. The encouraging report brought by Titus after a difficult situation (7:5-7)

> [5] For even when we came into Macedonia, our bodies had no rest, but we were afflicted in every way—disputes without and fears within. [6] But God, who consoles the downcast, consoled us by the arrival of Titus, [7] and not only by his coming, but also by the consolation with which he was consoled about you, as he told us of your longing, your mourning, your zeal for me, so that I rejoiced still more.

Paul begins in v. 5 by stressing that in Macedonia he found no rest, and "we were afflicted in every way." What afflicted him was both "disputes from

---

1. Guthrie, *2 Corinthians*, 368.

without" and "fears within." Any notion that the life of the Christian or Christian ministers is always rosy and peaceful is utterly foreign to Paul. After all, in his main section on authentic ministry (2:14—7:4) he had emphasized that authentic Christian faith and ministry had more than its fair share of hardships and was never plain sailing. At the end of v. 4 he had alluded to "all our affliction." When Timothy visited Corinth, probably in AD 54, he had taken a troubling report to Paul, and Paul had spoken of a troubling visit. In 2:4, he says that he wrote to Corinth "out of much distress and anguish of heart and with many tears." Paul would not have been human if he had not "fears within." One writer cites Charles H. Spurgeon as confessing that the trials of ministry were such that "I am the subject of such depressions of spirit, so fearful that I hope none of you ever gets to such extremes of wretchedness as I go to."[2]

In v. 6, Paul repeats almost what he said in 1:9, namely that "God, who consoles the downcast, consoled (Greek, *parakalōn*) us," this time by the arrival of Titus with good news and more (v. 7). Titus was a gentile convert to Christian faith, who became a fellow-worker whom Paul fully trusted, and who had accompanied Paul and Barnabas to Jerusalem. Titus reported the Corinthians' longing to see Paul. He had refrained from seeing them earlier (1:23), so this news was doubly welcome. Barrett suggests that a visiting missionary had attacked Paul, but that the Corinthians did not take his part. With gratitude he spoke of "your zeal for me" (v. 7). This made Paul "rejoice still more."

That the Corinthians had even entered into "mourning" shows that they had grasped the wrong that had been done to Paul. Thrall comments, "In consequence of these amended attitudes on their part Paul himself rejoices, rather than remaining in the earlier state of distress occasioned not only by his troubles in Macedonia but also (v. 8) by his doubts as to whether he should have written as he had done."[3]

Questions for reflection

1. Do we sometimes hold back when we should be showing "tough love"?

---

2. Guthrie, *2 Corinthians*, 373.
3. Thrall, *Second Corinthians*, 489.

2. The long-term positive effects of Paul's letter (7:8-13a)

⁸ For even if I made you sorry with my letter, I do not regret it (though I did regret it, for I see that I grieved you with that letter, though only briefly). ⁹ Now I rejoice, not because you were grieved, but because your grief led to repentance; for you felt a godly grief, so that you were not harmed in any way by us. ¹⁰ For godly grief produces a repentance that leads to salvation and brings no regret, but worldly grief produces death. ¹¹ For see what earnestness this godly grief has produced in you, what eagerness to clear yourselves, what indignation, what alarm, what longing, what zeal, what punishment! At every point you have proved yourselves guiltless in the matter. ¹² So although I wrote to you, it was not on account of the one who did the wrong, nor on account of the one who was wronged, but in order that your zeal for us might be made known to you before God. ¹³ In this we find comfort.

In v. 8, Paul admits that his letter made the Corinthians "sorry," but he only briefly had regrets. In retrospect, he is glad that he wrote it. His hesitation has given way to joy because of the effects that his letter finally achieved. He is sorry for the grief that the letter caused, but ultimately it succeeded in its purpose. Their grief led to their repentance (v. 9). Thrall suggests, "His rather involved preliminary remarks are perhaps intended as a partial apology for the pain he has caused. But the attempt at apology is soon given up."[4] She adds that the general sense is clear, even if the syntax is obscure and complex. This complexity gives rise to textual variation (v. 8).

First, "For I see (Greek, *blepō gar*) that I grieved you" (NRSV) has the present indicative with "for." Most MSS favor the present indicative (I see), as do Thrall, Harris, and Barrett. Second, the participle *blepōn* (seeing) is read by $\mathfrak{p}^{46}$, other Old Latin texts, and today the NEB and Hughes. Third, the reading *blepō* (I see, without "for") occurs in B, D*, and Syriac-Sahidic. Metzger notes that for once the Committee of the United Bible Society disagreed about the evaluation of the readings, the majority favoring "For I see," but admitting "a high degree of doubt."[5] These variants do not seriously affect the meaning, but witness to the complexity of the syntax and a scribe's attempt to correct it.

---

4. Thrall, *Second Corinthians*, 490.
5. Metzger, *A Textual Commentary on the Greek New Testament*, 512; Furnish, *II Corinthians*, 387; Thrall, *Second Corinthians*, 490-91; Harris, *Second Corinthians*, 533.

PART II: EXEGESIS

It is difficult to exaggerate the dramatic change in Paul's emotions after Titus had reported good news from Corinth. But he had had to do a hard thing by writing the letter, one of the most difficult things he had done in his ministry, and temporarily had initial regrets about it. But now he can put it in the past for it had achieved its original goal. The Corinthian church would not have reached its happy state without it. "Regret" (Greek, *metamelomai*) clearly implies a change of mind, and in other contexts may mean "to repent," even if *metanoeō* would be the usual word for this. Paul's admission of regret would have softened his earlier rebuke. Chrysostom compares the pain of surgery which may bring joy in the outcome.[6]

Paul now explains that the Corinthians' sadness, hurt, upset, or sorrow was willed by God, and nothing to do with Paul's "letting off steam" (v. 10). Their grief is different from worldly grief, which leads to disappointment or even death. Sorrow for sin is very different. Paul now recognizes how great an effect the experience of grief actually had on them. In v. 11, he uses seven terms to describe this difference: "earnestness, . . . eagerness to clear yourselves, . . . indignation, . . . alarm, . . . zeal, . . . punishment." *Earnestness* translates the Greek *spoudē*, which means quick action, diligence, or eager commitment. He uses the word again in v. 12 and 8:7.

Clearing of yourselves (v. 11) translates the Greek *apologia*, self-defense, sometimes in a court of law. *Indignation* translates *aganaktēsis*, and presumably refers to displeasure about how Paul had been treated. "Fear" (NRSV, alarm), may refer to fear of the Lord or reverence, or it may denote respect. *Zeal* (Greek, *zēlos*) probably means enthusiastic concern on Paul's behalf. *Longing* probably refers to longing to see Paul personally. Finally *punishment* translates the Greek *ekdikēsis*, which may not denote punishment here, but *justice*. In other contexts, it may denote *retaliation* or *vengeance*, but not here. It probably means the dispensing of justice. Danker renders *ekdikēsis, giving of justice, penalty inflicted on wrongdoers* or *punishment* (of Paul's opponents in 2 Cor 7:11).[7] All these seven responses demonstrate a total shift in the Corinthians' attitude to Paul. They have undergone a change of heart "at every point."

In v. 12, Paul anticipates the suspicion that he had been concerned only with his own personal feelings. Plummer writes, "His main object in writing was not to get the offender punished, or the person who was offended righted, but to give them an opportunity of showing how loyal they

---

6. Chrysostom, "Homily on 2 Corinthians," 350.
7. Danker, BDAG, 301.

really were to himself. We may regard it as almost certain that the person offended was himself."[8] This is one more allusion to the "severe" letter, which has been lost. Paul makes it clear that the injury was to the whole of the Corinthian church, not just to some individual. Some have suggested that the injured person might have been Timothy, but it is more likely to have been Paul. His letter showed what casting Paul off would mean for the church. That their zeal might be known "before God" stands in an emphatic position of solemnity. The first part of the next verse (v. 13a) concludes, "In this we find comfort" (Greek, *parakekklēmetha*).

Questions for reflection

1. Have we ever had to steel ourselves to say something hard to someone about whom we care? Are we tempted to avoid any kind of confrontation?
2. What has been the effect of "straight talking"? What has it achieved "in the sight of God"? Has the outcome been salutary and happy? If not, should we do something further, rather than allowing things to fester?

3. The joy of Titus at the Corinthians' response (7:13b–16)

> In addition to our own consolation, we rejoiced still more at the joy of Titus, because his mind has been set at rest by all of you. [14] For if I have been somewhat boastful about you to him, I was not disgraced; but just as everything we said to you was true, so our boasting to Titus has proved true as well. [15] And his heart goes out all the more to you, as he remembers the obedience of all of you, and how you welcomed him with fear and trembling. [16] I rejoice, because I have complete confidence in you.

The third and final movement of this section speaks of the joy of Titus after his encounter with the Corinthians. He actually found that his meeting with them had "set his mind at rest" or was refreshing (Greek, *anapepautai*, perfect passive, i.e., past with effects remaining). The NIV translates, "We are especially delighted to see how happy Titus was." This does good justice to the Greek *peissoterōs mallon echarēmen*, which uses a double comparative

---

8. Plummer, *Second Corinthians*, 224.

and redundant use of *mallon* with *perissoterōs*, i.e., *more abundantly*. The implication is that Titus, acting on behalf of Paul, was relieved and proud of the outcome of his labors in Corinth. Titus' joy is contagious.

In v. 14, Paul had "boasted" to Titus that the situation in Corinth would reflect the work of God. If it relates to what God has done, Christians should not be reluctant to boast or express pride in a situation. Paul is not boasting in some personal accomplishment. He would have been shamed (or "disgraced," NRSV, v. 14) if the outcome had been reversed. His special concern for Titus reminds us that Paul always ministered with fellow workers collaboratively. He was no solitary loner.[9]

The affection of Titus for the Corinthians has been established, and Paul shares that affection. He is not only affectionate, but also confident in them. The Greek *tharreō* expresses that confidence; it expresses joy, courage, and hope. It sets in contrast the "fear and trembling" that was once felt.

Questions for reflection

1. Do we sufficiently think of Paul as a team player? Do we value and encourage collaborative ministry? Or do we expect one single leader to do everything?

2. Do we allow ourselves to take pride in someone else's work when it is clearly God's work?

---

9. Ollrog, *Paulus und seine Mitarbeiter*; Ellis, "Paul and his Co-workers"; Harrington, "Paul and Collaborative Ministry"; Bruce, *The Pauline Circle*.

V

THE COLLECTION FOR POOR CHRISTIANS IN JERUSALEM

8:1—9:15

1. Paul's exhortation to finish the collection (8:1-15)

¹ We want you to know, brothers and sisters, about the grace of God that has been granted to the churches of Macedonia; ² for during a severe ordeal of affliction, their abundant joy and their extreme poverty have overflowed in a wealth of generosity on their part. ³ For, as I can testify, they voluntarily gave according to their means, and even beyond their means, ⁴ begging us earnestly for the privilege of sharing in this ministry to the saints— ⁵ and this, not merely as we expected; they gave themselves first to the Lord and, by the will of God, to us, ⁶ so that we might urge Titus that, as he had already made a beginning, so he should also complete this generous undertaking among you. ⁷ Now as you excel in everything—in faith, in speech, in knowledge, in utmost eagerness, and in our love for you—so we want you to excel also in this generous undertaking.

⁸ I do not say this as a command, but I am testing the genuineness of your love against the earnestness of others. ⁹ For you know the generous act of our Lord Jesus Christ, that though he was rich, yet for your sakes he became poor, so that by his poverty you might become rich. ¹⁰ And in this matter I am giving my advice: it is appropriate for you who began last year not only to do something but even to desire to do something— ¹¹ now finish doing it, so that your eagerness may be matched by completing it according to your means. ¹² For if the eagerness is there, the gift is acceptable according to what one has—not according to what

one does not have. ¹³ I do not mean that there should be relief for others and pressure on you, but it is a question of a fair balance between ¹⁴ your present abundance and their need, so that their abundance may be for your need, in order that there may be a fair balance. ¹⁵ As it is written,

> "The one who had much did not have too much,
> and the one who had little did not have too little."

The first section (8:1–15) presents the Macedonians as an example of exceptionally generous giving. The second (8:16—9:5) focuses on Titus and his eagerness to travel to Corinth again. The third (9:6–15) presents Paul's further reflections on giving to God's work for the blessing of other Christians. Thrall includes chapter 8 as a unity with chapters with 1–7 but classifies chapter 9 and chapters 10–13 as separate letters, with chapters 10–13 being the otherwise "lost" "painful letter."[1] Although we may not be fully convinced by the identification of chapters 10–13 with the painful letter, there are admittedly plausible reasons for the theory. In 2:3 Paul speaks of having written a previous letter; in 1:23 he speaks of abandoning a proposed visit, while in 13:2 a visit is in prospect; and in 2:9 he implies satisfaction with the Corinthians' obedience, while in 10:6 this "obedience" has yet to be completed.

Thrall, Betz, and Bultmann believe that chapters 8 and 9 belong to different letters, although both from Paul.[2] Bultmann regards Paul's motive in chapter 8 as "the promise of Gal 2:10," and his motive in chapter 9 as "the honor of Paul and the community."[3] Nevertheless, Thrall also admits, "In content chaps. 8 and 9 belong together."[4] Harris also includes careful arguments that the chapters 8 and 9 "belong together," with "a network of specific links."[5] Supposedly 8:20 and 9:3–5 imply two differing purposes for the sending of the collection to Jerusalem, as Bultmann argues. But more than half a dozen respected scholars, including Furnish, Martin, Witherington, and Hall, retain their belief in the unity of 2 Cor 1–9, although Martin agrees that chapter 8 might have originally been sent separately to Corinth, whereas chapter 9 is intended for a wider

---

1. Thrall, *Second Corinthians*, 503 and vol. 1, 13–18.
2. Thrall, *Second Corinthians*, 564; Betz and MacRae, *2 Corinthians 8 and 9*; Bultmann, *Second Corinthians*, 253–58.
3. Bultmann, *Second Corinthians*, 253 and 257.
4. Thrall, *Second Corinthians*, 504.
5. Harris, *Second Corinthians*, 27–29.

circle in Achaia.[6] This may depend on whether the brothers of 8:18, 24 are the same as the brothers of 9:3. Further, are "the saints" of 8:4 the same as "the saints" of 9:1?

In 8:1, Paul wants the Corinthians to be aware of a specific expression of God's grace evidenced in the churches of Macedonia. These included the churches of Philippi, Thessalonica, and Beroea, i.e., the "Romanized" centers. Philippi was, like Corinth, a Roman colony, and Thessalonica and Beroea were "*municipia*."[7] "Grace" (Greek, *charis*) is used more widely as the basis of the ministry of Jesus Christ and of the whole Christian life; but here the term is used more narrowly as the gift or favor which is exemplified in the sacrificial generosity of the Macedonian churches.[8] Guthrie notes the tragic contrast of most Western churches today, which are "drowning in wealth" and yet often show a poverty of giving to other churches in need.[9]

Paul goes into a more detailed explanation of the situation in 8:2-5. The generosity of the Macedonians described in his examples is elaborate. Their giving was extraordinary on top of "a severe ordeal of affliction" and "extreme poverty" (Greek, *hē kata bathous ptōcheia autōn*) (v. 2). The Greek *ptōcheia* derives from *ptōcheuō*, which once meant *to be a beggar*.[10] The generosity of the Macedonians, described in his examples, is extensive. Thrall comments that opinions differ about the cause of their poverty, but it is "probable that their poverty was due to social ostracism and harassment on account of their new faith."[11] Their poverty and joy might seem paradoxical, but their experience of poverty led them to be sympathetic with their brothers who were also poor. The Greek *haplotēs* ought to mean "generosity" in this context, but it usually means simplicity, frankness, or sincerity. However, it can mean generosity, as in Rom 12:8.[12] They gave under difficult circumstances (cf. Acts 17:5-8; Phil 1:28-30; 1 Thess 1:6; 2:14; 3:3-4). They gave extravagantly in spite of their extreme poverty.

---

6. Furnish, *II Corinthians*, 41-44; Martin, *2 Corinthians*, xxxvi and xlv-xlvi and 249-50; Witherington, *Conflict and Community in Corinth*, 411-14; Plummer, *Second Corinthians*, xix-xx; Hughes, *Second Corinthians*, xxi-xxxv; Hall, *The Unity of the Corinthian Correspondence*, 114-19.

7. Betz, *2 Corinthians 8 and 9*, 49-53; Thrall, *Second Corinthians*, 521.

8. Danker, BDAG, 1079-80.

9. Guthrie, *2 Corinthians*, 393.

10. Robertson, *Word Pictures*, vol. 4, 243.

11. Thrall, *Second Corinthians*, 523.

12. Danker, BDAG, 104.

PART II: EXEGESIS

The word often translated "overflow" (Greek, *perisseuō*) occurs ten times in 2 Corinthians, three times in chapter 8, and three times in chapter 9. It reflects the terms "abounding," "abundance," and even "superabundance." The Macedonian churches gave voluntarily and quite beyond their resources. In vv. 3–4, Paul is eager to stress the extent and spontaneity of their response to the needs of the Jerusalem church. Such is Paul's eagerness that he omits the main verb, "they gave," although it is understood in the grammar. Thrall rightly comments that this may have been to allay possible suspicions that the giving was due to apostolic pressure.[13] Their motive was service to God and to other people, i.e., sharing (Greek, *koinonia*) in the relief project. Thrall comments, "The Macedonians begged (Greek, *deomai*) the favor of participation in the *diakonia*" (ministry).[14]

J. N. Collins and Betz understand Greek *diakonia* (ministry) to relate to the administration of the money raised for the Jerusalem church.[15] Collins renders *diakonia* as "mission" here, but if we render it as "participation" or "sharing," this more naturally refers to the ministry of giving rather than "administration" and accompanying Paul on his journey to Jerusalem. They responded with what they had to give. Giving by the extremely poor rather than the rich seems such a surprise that Paul adds "as I can testify" (Greek, *marturō*, v. 3). In v. 5, Paul expresses his surprise: "not merely as we expected." We may note that the Macedonians gave not only money but "themselves." The total self-giving also delighted Paul. "First" is not temporal but means "of first importance."

In v. 6, Paul moves on to encourage the Corinthians to emulate the example of the Macedonians churches. He therefore wants to build on Titus' success in Corinth. Furnish points out that Titus had "already made a beginning" in taking up an offering from the Corinthians for the poor in Jerusalem, but that there is no evidence that Titus' attempt predated 1 Cor 16:1–4.[16] The visit of Titus simply encouraged Paul to hope for something more. Now in v. 7 he makes an explicit appeal: "We want you to excel also in this generous undertaking."

Paul hopes that the generosity of the church in Corinth will match their faith, speech, knowledge, and eagerness. These qualities were evident in 1 Corinthians as well as in the visit of Titus. Pogoloff, Engels, Theissen, I,

13. Thrall, *Second Corinthians*, 525.
14. Thrall, *Second Corinthians*, 525.
15. Collins, *Diakonia*, 218 and 336.
16. Furnish, *II Corinthians*, 414.

and others have stressed this.[17] In view of such flourishing trade and business contacts (see Introduction), the church in Corinth would be unlikely to suffer such dire poverty as some of the churches of Macedonia. It has been noteworthy, however, that throughout the history of the church, the poorest churches have often been most generous in giving to those in need. This still applies today to many churches in Africa. The verb "to complete" (v. 6, *epiteleō*) or "to finish" corresponds to "begin" (Greek, *anarchomai*).

In v. 8, Paul assures the Corinthians that he does not want to tell them as a command (Greek, *epitagē*) to contribute to the collection because he wants this to be voluntary. This is what he means by "testing (Greek, *dokimazō*) the genuineness of your love." "Genuineness" means *true* or *legitimate*.[18] This verse, among others, questions Castelli's notion that Paul is authoritarian. This is why he appeals to them to reflect the enthusiasm (Greek, *spoudē*) and love of the Macedonian churches.

Paul cites an even more profound example than the Macedonians in v. 9. He appeals to the example of Jesus Christ himself. Similarly to what he will later say in Phil 2:5-11, Christ, though he was rich, became poor for our sake "that by his poverty you might become rich" (v. 9). Chrysostom comments that the belief that poverty can generate wealth is shown in the example of Jesus Christ.[19] The grace of God was embodied in Jesus of Nazareth. Christians are called to share Christ's magnanimity.

Paul repeats his words about voluntary giving in v. 10. He explicitly calls this his "advice" (Greek, *gnōmē*). Furnish translates this as "counsel" or "considered opinion."[20] But in v. 11 he returns to an imperative: "finish doing it." Paul also shows that "It is not the size of their gift that makes it acceptable, but their goodwill in giving as their resources allow (v. 12)."[21] The Corinthians are not expected to give more than they are able.

Paul clarifies the principle of proportionate giving in vv. 13-15. Furnish, Guthrie, and Thrall call this section the principle of equality; Hughes calls it "a law of equilibrium."[22] The Greek phrase is *ex isotētos*,

---

17. Pogoloff, *Logos and Sophia*, throughout; Engels, *Roman Corinth*, 8-143; Theissen, *The Social Setting of Pauline Christianity*, 69-174; Thiselton, *The First Epistle to the Corinthians*, 1-29, and throughout.

18. Danker, BDAG, 202.

19. Chrysostom, "Homilies in the Second Epistle to the Corinthians," Hom. 17, 360.

20. Furnish, *II Corinthians*, 405.

21. Furnish, *II Corinthians*, 419.

22. Hughes, *Second Corinthians*, 306.

equal, from an older word, *fair* or *equal*.[23] Martin includes an additional note on the Pauline Collection, which traces Paul's sense of responsibility as part of his agreement made in Jerusalem according to Gal 2:10 cf. 1 Cor 16:1–4; 2 Cor 8 and 9; Rom 15:27–29.[24] The reason for the poverty of the church in Jerusalem, he says, can only be guessed. Karl Holl and Dieter Georgi have written at length on the subject of the collection.[25] NRSV's "that there may be a fair balance" is rendered by Guthrie "This is how equality works" (v. 14). The situation of surplus is compared with need "at the present time." This principle of reciprocity was important in the Greco-Roman world. Both parties have their obligations. But Paul appeals to equality among Christians.

Paul cites Exod 16:18 in v. 15, where God provided manna for the Israelites during the time of the wilderness wanderings. Each person was to gather only enough for personal needs, and not to hoard it. It was a day-by-day provision for a day-to-day need. Hence: "The one who had much did not have too much; and the one who had little did not have too little" (v. 15). This lays down a principle of how God's people are to treat one another. This broadly reflects what Paul has said about "one body" in 1 Cor 12. The appeal for the poor in Jerusalem becomes a universal principle for all churches.

Questions for reflection

1. The churches of Macedonia (including Philippi, Thessalonica, and Beroea) had proved themselves an outstanding example of generosity. Yet they were undergoing "extreme poverty." Why is it that so often the poorest churches seem to excel in generous giving? What does this say about the modern West?

2. Can we imagine "begging for the privilege" of giving? Is our desire to give to others spontaneous or grudging and dutiful?

3. To what extent is our motivation to give influenced by Jesus Christ, who, though he was rich, became poor?

---

23. Robertson, *Word Pictures*, vol. 4, 245.

24. Martin, *2 Corinthians*, 256–58.

25. Georgi, *Remembering the Poor*; Holl, "Der Kirchenbegriff des Paulus in seinem Verhältnis zu dem der Urgemeinde."

4. Do we take seriously the principle of a "fair balance" among fellow-Christians or churches? Is our church a "wealthy" church or one that reaches out to help no matter what our financial situation?

2. Titus' eagerness to travel to Corinth again (8:16—9:5)

¹⁶ But thanks be to God who put in the heart of Titus the same eagerness for you that I myself have. ¹⁷ For he not only accepted our appeal, but since he is more eager than ever, he is going to you of his own accord. ¹⁸ With him we are sending the brother who is famous among all the churches for his proclaiming the good news; ¹⁹ and not only that, but he has also been appointed by the churches to travel with us while we are administering this generous undertaking for the glory of the Lord himself and to show our goodwill. ²⁰ We intend that no one should blame us about this generous gift that we are administering, ²¹ for we intend to do what is right not only in the Lord's sight but also in the sight of others. ²² And with them we are sending our brother whom we have often tested and found eager in many matters, but who is now more eager than ever because of his great confidence in you. ²³ As for Titus, he is my partner and co-worker in your service; as for our brothers, they are messengers of the churches, the glory of Christ. ²⁴ Therefore openly before the churches, show them the proof of your love and of our reason for boasting about you.

9 Now it is not necessary for me to write you about the ministry to the saints, ² for I know your eagerness, which is the subject of my boasting about you to the people of Macedonia, saying that Achaia has been ready since last year; and your zeal has stirred up most of them. ³ But I am sending the brothers in order that our boasting about you may not prove to have been empty in this case, so that you may be ready, as I said you would be; ⁴ otherwise, if some Macedonians come with me and find that you are not ready, we would be humiliated—to say nothing of you—in this undertaking. ⁵ So I thought it necessary to urge the brothers to go on ahead to you, and arrange in advance for this bountiful gift that you have promised, so that it may be ready as a voluntary gift and not as an extortion.

In vv. 16–24, Paul explains that Titus is the local envoy on the mission team with two others. 9:1–5 explains the purpose of the mission. We have already discussed why we are convinced about the unity of chapters 8 and 9.

Paul repeats what he has said about the eagerness of Titus to visit Corinth again, stressing that it is God who had inspired this eagerness in Titus, and that Paul shares his eagerness. Titus is even going "of his own accord" (v. 17). Thrall comments in her very detailed commentary that this needs no further explanation.[26] Paul uses the word "appeal," she suggests, because he is a "leader who makes requests rather than giving orders."[27] Betz calls Titus "a legal mandate" but this seems more formal, directive, and influenced by Rome than the text implies.

Some suggest that Titus has already left for Corinth, but this is unlikely. In v. 18, Paul adds a second brother who will accompany Titus, who is "famous among all the churches for proclaiming the good news." Moreover, he was appointed by the churches to travel with Paul's party while they were administering this generous undertaking (v. 19). Some prefer the translation "elected" (Greek, *cheirotonein*), which "originally meant 'to elect by a show of hands.'"[28] Thrall and the JB also read "elect." She suggests that Paul may have initiated the election, although the precise identity of the churches is uncertain. The result of this election or appointment is to increase Paul's own eagerness for the delegation. Most writers conclude that the brothers cannot be identified with certainty. Some have suggested Barnabas, Luke, Sopater, and others, but most writers reject these speculations. Above all, it is "for the glory of the Lord himself."

The good reputation of the brother leads to Paul's defending his own reputation once again in v. 20: "that no one should blame us about this generous gift that we are administering." Why should anyone blame Paul? The target of possible accusation seems to depend on what is suggested about Paul's motive. Paul had already defended himself against charges of seeking financial support in 1 Cor 9:4-18. Barrett comments, "Paul could hardly hope to avoid the charge that he was enriching himself by his missionary work; few evangelists have avoided it."[29] Paul does not explicitly cite a Scriptural passage, but Prov 3:4 (LXX) seems to lie behind the phrase "not only in the Lord's sight but also in the sight of others" (v. 21), as Thrall, Barrett, and others believe. He reinforces his attitude of integrity. Verse 22 underlines Paul's collegiality and his customary association with fellow-workers.

---

26. Thrall, *Second Corinthians*, 544.
27. Thrall, *Second Corinthians*, 545.
28. Furnish, *II Corinthians*, 422.
29. Barrett, *Second Corinthians*, 229.

In v. 23, "Paul summarizes the basic credentials of his three envoys, distinguished somewhat between Titus . . . and the other two."[30] Titus is explicitly called his fellow-worker (Greek, *synergos*) or his partner. Betz uses the term "administrative assistant," or "authorized representative," which might serve business contexts, but Thrall doubts whether this interpretation can be substantiated.[31] In the concluding verse of this chapter (v. 24), "Paul urges his readers to give proof both of their own Christian love and also of the validity of his boasting about them."[32] Thrall includes an excursus on the brothers of chapter 8.[33]

On chapter 9 as a whole, Thrall writes, "Paul is more than a little apprehensive about the adequacy of the Corinthians activity in respect of the collection. . . . The envoys are to make sure that the Corinthian contribution is ready before Paul arrives in person."[34] Although Betz, Bultmann, and Thrall (more tentatively) regard chapter 9 as a separate letter, it is still Pauline, and we have argued that the case for distinct letters is far from proven. Betz writes bluntly, "Paul figured that his readers were so familiar with the subject of the collection that they had grown tired of hearing of it. Rhetorically speaking, the collection might have become a matter of supposed 'boredom' or 'weariness.'"[35] However, we noted that there are many links between chapters 8 and 9. In 9:1, Paul admits that his writing further on the collection may be redundant: "It is not necessary for me to write." The Greek *peri men gar* (literally "for concerning") is simply rendered as "now" in the NRSV. This is probably helpful, but Betz makes much of it to support his argument that chapters 8 and 9 are separate "administrative" letters. Stanley Stowers has argued convincingly that the Greek phrase has been used to indicate a close connection with what precedes it.[36]

Paul confirms that Achaea has been prepared since last year, and now uses the readiness of Corinth to encourage the Macedonian churches (9:2), just as in 8:1, 8, he used the generosity of the Macedonians to encourage the church or churches in Corinth. Barrett comments that vv. 3-4 "show that Paul was already somewhat embarrassed and feared further

---

30. Thrall, *Second Corinthians*, 553.
31. Betz, *2 Corinthians 8 and 9*, 79-80; Thrall, *Second Corinthians*, 553.
32. Thrall, *Second Corinthians*, 556
33. Thrall, *Second Corinthians*, 557-62
34. Thrall, *Second Corinthians*, 557-62.
35. Betz, *2 Corinthians 8 and 9*, 90.
36. Stowers, *"Peri Men Gar* and the Integrity of 2 Corinthians 8 and 9."

embarrassment."[37] He further notes that Paul was in the habit of seeing the best in his people and presented them in this light to others. After attempting to suggest that the Macedonian churches and Corinthian Christians should emulate each other in generosity, it would constitute a tragic anti-climax if the Macedonians were to arrive in Achaea only to find that the delegation and mission were still not organized. Partly for this reason, Hughes suggests, Paul wanted to send Titus, who was Macedonian, to accompany the delegates.[38] Paul intended to follow Titus.

Betz comments, "The section vv. 3–5b consists of a report by Paul justifying his inclusion of the two brothers in the delegation to Corinth."[39] He adds, "All too familiar with the situation in Corinth, the Achaeans might have begun to worry that the inclusion of the two brothers signalled a fresh outbreak of trouble."[40] But Paul turns to the Achaeans for help. Guthrie observes, "Paul is walking a fine line here. He wants to acknowledge and affirm what can be affirmed, while at the same time offering appropriate encouragement to get on with the process."[41] This explains what might otherwise look like repetition. Hughes comments, "Our examination of the first five verses of chapter 9 has shown that they are not at all superfluous, but supplementary to what is said in 8:16–24 concerning the mission of the advance-party who preceded Paul to Corinth."[42] Chapter 9 presumes that the visit is impending; chapter 8 (perhaps a few weeks earlier) urges that this mission is still to be completed.[43]

The United Bible Society Committee disagreed about the MS reading of 9:4. The early $\mathfrak{p}^{46}$, C*, D, and others agreed in favoring Greek singular (*I say*, or "to say nothing of you"); but B and other MSS read the plural (*we say*). According to Metzger, a majority of the UBS Committee supported $\mathfrak{p}^{46}$ C*, D, and G (Western text), explaining the plural as scribal assimilation.[44] The practical difference is minimal. In 9:5, Paul summarizes three points: that the visit is necessary (Greek, *anankaion*); that practical organization is needed; and that the Corinthians' generous gift will be ready and given with

37. Barrett, *Second Corinthians*, 233.
38. Hughes, *Second Corinthians*, 326.
39. Betz, *2 Corinthians 8 and 9*, 93.
40. Betz, *2 Corinthians 8 and 9*, 94.
41. Guthrie, *2 Corinthians*, 434.
42. Hughes, *Second Corinthians*, 327.
43. Furnish, *II Corinthians*, 431.
44. Metzger, *Textual Commentary*, 514.

the right attitude. The collection itself is "your blessing" (Greek, *eulogian humōn*), translated as "your bountiful gift" (NRSV).

Questions for reflection

1. Although he was eager to visit Corinth, Titus could not have known how his visit to Corinth would turn out. In the event, it turned out that God blessed it far beyond all expectations. Do we sometimes waste needless anxiety on whether what God has planned will be a wonderful blessing?
2. Paul's sending ahead of the three brothers proved to be the right thing. Do we ever blunder in, when more preparation might lead to a better outcome?
3. A delegation from the Macedonian and Corinthian churches would have been more impressive than a single church. Do our churches sufficiently act together?

3. Wider reflections on giving and the generosity of God (9:6–15)

⁶ The point is this: the one who sows sparingly will also reap sparingly, and the one who sows bountifully will also reap bountifully. ⁷ Each of you must give as you have made up your mind, not reluctantly or under compulsion, for God loves a cheerful giver. ⁸ And God is able to provide you with every blessing in abundance, so that by always having enough of everything, you may share abundantly in every good work. ⁹ As it is written,

> "He scatters abroad, he gives to the poor;
> his righteousness endures forever."

¹⁰ He who supplies seed to the sower and bread for food will supply and multiply your seed for sowing and increase the harvest of your righteousness. ¹¹ You will be enriched in every way for your great generosity, which will produce thanksgiving to God through us; ¹² for the rendering of this ministry not only supplies the needs of the saints but also overflows with many thanksgivings to God. ¹³ Through the testing of this ministry you glorify God by your obedience to the confession of the gospel of Christ and by the generosity of your sharing with them and with all others, ¹⁴ while

they long for you and pray for you because of the surpassing grace of God that he has given you. ¹⁵ Thanks be to God for his indescribable gift!

The NRSV and Thrall helpfully render the Greek *touto de*—a non-verbal, elliptical expression—by "The point is this . . . ." Some suggest an alternative rendering: "Now think about this" or "Now remember this law" (Plummer). The phrase introduces what follows. The point is wider and more general. One reaps, Paul says, what one sows. The principle is expressed in Prov 22:8 and Job 4:8 and constitutes a saying in the Wisdom tradition. Paul quotes it in Gal 6:7. Thrall cites applications of the saying not only in the Old Testament, but also in Aristotle, Cicero, Philo, and others. The proverb was well known in the Greco-Roman world. Paul applies it to sowing sparingly (Greek, *pheidomenos*) and bountifully or generously (Greek, *ep' eulogiais*). This phrase looks back to the description of the Macedonian Christians' gift as generous. The church father Ambrosiaster describes those who sow sparingly as "misers."[45] The contrasting term to "tight-fisted" means "open-handed" or the heart's desire to bless others. How we sow leads proportionately to what kind of harvest we may expect.

Plummer comments that vv. 6–15 "are a closely united whole."[46] It is concerned not only with giving, but with giving in a right spirit. Such giving is sure of a good harvest. In v. 7, Paul explains that God loves a cheerful giver, not one who gives reluctantly or grudgingly. However, as Thrall comments, this does not mean that God loves *only* a cheerful giver.[47] Hence, the one who gives must "make up his mind" on what he should give. The emphasis is on lack of compulsion. The language is similar to that of Epictetus (broadly contemporary with Paul), but this does not imply conscious dependence on him.

Paul further explains in vv. 8–11 that God blesses generous givers. One important word in v. 8 is "able" (Greek, *dynatei*). God is *able* to make all things abound to you. Other important words include "every" blessing (Greek, *pasan*), "in abundance" (Greek verb, *perisseusai*), "in everything" and "always" (Greek, *en panti* and *pantote*), again, "everything" (Greek, *pasan autarkean*), and again "abound" (Greek, *perisseuēte*). In other

---

45. Ambrosiaster, *Commentary on Paul's Epistles*, cited in Gerald Bray (ed.), *1–2 Corinthians*, 279.

46. Plummer, *Second Corinthians*, 257.

47. Thrall, *Second Corinthians*, 576.

words, Paul uses alliteration to voice at least six times the letter "p" (Greek letter, π) to emphasize the point rhetorically.[48]

Paul cites Scripture (Ps 111:9, LXX) in v. 9. The person who "scatters abroad" and gives to the poor, "his righteousness endures forever." In the original psalm, the subject is the pious, beneficent person.[49] But some suggest that here God is the subject, as in v. 8. Hanson refers it to Christ in the Christian.[50] Paul continues to stress God's abundant provision of resources in v. 10, in spite of minor textual variants in the following verbs. God will supply and multiply seed for sowing and bread for food. Frances Young and David Ford provide a hermeneutical and pastorally sensitive exposition of the abundance of God for the church in their *Meaning and Truth in 2 Corinthians*.

Paul repeats his assertion that God will abundantly enrich the Corinthian Christians in v. 11. There will be an increase in both their economic and spiritual wealth, and this generosity will produce thanksgiving to God. In v. 12, Paul stresses that the outburst of thanksgiving flows from the meeting of needs for the church in Jerusalem. Paul hoped and expected that the generosity of the Corinthians would outstrip that of the Macedonian churches.

The offering of prayer to God becomes the theme of 9:12–15. This section focuses on the effects of the giving. These consist of (i) thanksgiving to God (v. 12); (ii) giving glory to God (v. 13); and (iii) prayer offered for the Corinthian churches (v. 14). In v. 12, the ministry (Greek, *diakonia*) of generous giving "overflows (or abounds) with many thanksgivings to God." Here "ministry" may denote a wider service than giving alone. In v. 13, Paul speaks of the effect of glorifying God. "Glorifying" (Greek, *doxazontes*) is a nominative participle. Betz translates 9:13 as "Through the evidence of this charitable gift, they praise God for the submission [expressed] by the generosity of the partnership benefiting them and all."[51] This flows from the "testing of this ministry" (NRSV) or perhaps from its "proven character" (Greek, *tēs dokimēs*). God is glorified "by your obedience" (Greek, *hypotagēi*), a rare word derived from *hypotassō*, I obey or submit.

The exact meaning of "confession" in v. 13 is controversial. Betz pursues his distinctive argument that the term is entirely legal, meaning "contractual

48. Guthrie, *2 Corinthians*, 451; Robertson, *Word Pictures*, vol. 4, 249.
49. Thrall, *Second Corinthians*, 580.
50. Hanson, *Studies in Paul's Technique and Theology*, 179–80.
51. Betz, *2 Corinthians 8 and 9*, 87.

PART II: EXEGESIS

agreement."[52] He admits that "it does not mean 'confession' as a ritual act" or in its normal sense in the New Testament.[53] He writes, "We conclude that Paul's language reflects the language of a document which would have to be called a *homologia*."[54] Betz's proposal might just be plausible if we find sufficient evidence for this meaning in the New Testament. But it also belongs to a wider case for the meaning of "obedience" (Greek, *hypotagē*). He argues that the contractual agreement establishes the dominance of the Jerusalem church in relation to the gentile Christian communities. The collection creates this agreement between the churches.

Thrall and many others, however, dispute Betz's interpretation. They regard "confession" as used in its traditional sense. *Confession* in the New Testament is normally the open or public declaration of faith, as Cullmann and Neufeld point out.[55] This declaration may take the form of word and/or deed. Thrall comments, "The Jerusalem Christians glorify God because of the conversion of the Gentiles whose gifts were delivered to them. The collection is proof that these Gentiles too have been brought to 'the obedience of faith' (Rom 1:5)."[56] She concludes, "Other New Testament occurrences of *homologia* (6:12–13; Heb. 3:1; 4:14; 10:23) in no way support the sense Betz wishes to give to it in the present verse, nor do the two Pauline instances of *homologeō* suggest it."[57] Similarly Guthrie understands "obedience" to mean obedience to the gospel.[58]

"While they long for you" (v. 14, Greek, *autōn epipothountōn*) is genitive absolute (the "while clause" as a participle) with the participle standing for a finite verb, as NRSV translates it.[59] Paul uses the verb to denote affection. These are prayers of longing. The clause "and pray for you" (Greek, *deēsei*, dative) could mean "in prayer" or "by prayer." The preposition *dia* with the accusative indicates that this prayer is because God's extraordinary grace rests on you, or "because of the surpassing grace of God that he has given you" (NRSV). "Grace" (Greek, *charis*) remains a constant theme of this epistle.

---

52. Betz, *2 Corinthians 8 and 9*, 122–29.
53. Betz, *2 Corinthians 8 and 9*, 123.
54. Betz, *2 Corinthians 8 and 9*, 125.
55. Cullmann, *The Earliest Christian Confessions*, 10–34; Neufeld, *The Earliest Christian Confessions*, 7–33 and 42–68.
56. Thrall, *Second Corinthians*, 589.
57. Thrall, *Second Corinthians*, 590.
58. Guthrie, *2 Corinthians*, 459.
59. Guthrie, *2 Corinthians*, 460 and Robertson, *Word Pictures*, vol. 4, 250.

This section ends with an exclamatory expression of thanks to God: "Thanks be to God for his indescribable gift!" (NRSV, NIV, New English Bible, v. 15). The Greek word *anekdiēgētō* occurs only here in biblical literature, and twice later in Clement of Rome (c.95 AD) to mean the indescribable wonder of God's judgments (1 Clem. 20:5; 61:1). Furnish sees the indescribable gift as God's grace at work among the Macedonian churches, while Plummer sees this as the loving unity between Jewish and gentile Christians, and Martin, as the foundational grace of God that makes the gospel possible.[60] Barrett sees it as the gift of justification by grace.[61] Thrall comments, "It is not surprising that he [Paul] should conclude with a climactic and liturgical-sounding expression of gratitude to God for his indescribable gift."[62] She asks, however, whether it is specially the grace of God operative in the collection or the gift of Christ. She concludes, "It is the supreme gift of Christ that is meant."[63] It is emphatically *God's* gift, as the Father who gave his Son.

Questions for reflection

1. How seriously do we take to heart that a person reaps what they have sown? Is this a warning or an encouragement, or both?
2. Are there principles, sayings, or proverbs in society as a whole that we should heed?
3. Since God loves a cheerful giver, what does this say about our motives in being too tight-fisted or open-handed in our giving?
4. Do our actions testify to our confession of the gospel?
5. Are there examples of generous giving that inspire us to do likewise?
6. For what indescribable gift are we most ready to thank God?

---

60. Plummer, *Second Corinthians*, 267–68; Furnish, *II Corinthians*, 452; Martin, *2 Corinthians*, 295.
61. Barrett, *Second Corinthians*, 241–42.
62. Thrall, *Second Corinthians*, 594.
63. Thrall, *Second Corinthians*, 594.

VI

PAUL CONFRONTS THE HOSTILE MINISTRY OF HIS OPPONENTS

10:1—13:13

As we observed in our Introduction, the most decisive question about the unity of 2 Corinthians is the alleged break between chapters 1–9 and chapters 10–13. Thrall observes, "The last four chapters of the canonical 2 Corinthians have aroused critical attention for more than two centuries."[1] 2 Corinthians 10:1 begins with "I, Paul, myself," and in 10:2 he attacks "some," in 10:11 "such people," and later "those who want an opportunity to be recognized as our equals in what they boast about" (11:12), "false apostles" (11:13), and "servants of Satan," "who disguise themselves as servants of righteousness" (11:15). Many writers argue that, in Kümmel's words, this reflects "a completely different position of Paul in respect of the church from that in II. [chapters] 1–9."[2] He cites some thirteen scholars who regard chapters 10–13 as an "intermediate" epistle dating from the period between 1 and 2 Corinthians.

Kümmel considers that "it is hardly possible that II [chapters] 1–9 and II [chapters] 10–13 were dictated one right after the other," but adds, "It cannot be declared as inconceivable that Paul, after a certain interval of time, added to the epistle a conclusion in which he expressed more sharply his continuing concern for the congregation."[3] We should be cautious, he concludes, about premature decisions on this question. Munck argues that Paul received fresh concerning reports; Lietzmann, that Paul had a sleepless

---

1. Thrall, *Second Corinthians*, 595.
2. Kümmel, *Introduction to the New Testament*, 212.
3. Kümmel, *Introduction to the New Testament*, 213.

night; and so on. Furnish (1984) argued for the unity of the epistle; Young and Ford (1987) argued for its unity; Martin (1991); Witherington (1995); Hall (2003); Harris (2005); and Guthrie (2015); have all thrown their combined weight against theories of partition.

We strongly affirm their arguments, in spite of plausible claims on the other side. Most recently Guthrie has traced many connections between the two contested sections, concluding, "The apostle held in reserve a very direct and confrontive word to the opponents until the very end of the letter and did so for the rhetorical impact."[4] Barrett writes, "The only explanation of the new tone in x–xii is that Paul had heard further news from Corinth—not that the situation had changed completely but that it had developed. Such news could have arrived while he was writing; he could have decided to let what he had written stand and simply add a supplement."[5]

1. Present or absent, Paul's authority is the same: his response to criticism (10:1–11)

I myself, Paul, appeal to you by the meekness and gentleness of Christ—I who am humble when face to face with you, but bold toward you when I am away!— [2] I ask that when I am present I need not show boldness by daring to oppose those who think we are acting according to human standards. [3] Indeed, we live as human beings, but we do not wage war according to human standards; [4] for the weapons of our warfare are not merely human, but they have divine power to destroy strongholds. We destroy arguments [5] and every proud obstacle raised up against the knowledge of God, and we take every thought captive to obey Christ. [6] We are ready to punish every disobedience when your obedience is complete.

[7] Look at what is before your eyes. If you are confident that you belong to Christ, remind yourself of this, that just as you belong to Christ, so also do we. [8] Now, even if I boast a little too much of our authority, which the Lord gave for building you up and not for tearing you down, I will not be ashamed of it. [9] I do not want to seem as though I am trying to frighten you with my letters. [10] For they say, "His letters are weighty and strong, but his bodily presence is weak, and his speech contemptible." [11] Let such

---

4. Guthrie, *2 Corinthians*, 464.
5. Barrett, *Second Corinthians*, 244.

people understand that what we say by letter when absent, we will also do when present.

Paul begins, "I, Paul, myself, appeal (Greek, *parakalō*) to you." Bjerkelund argues in his book *Parakalō* that the verb denotes something a little stronger than "please" but falls definitely short of "I command." It means *appeal*, *beseech*, or *request*, but with both moral discernment or moral authority and respect for the spiritual independence of the addressees.[6] Paul's approach is with confidence but also with the meekness and gentleness of Christ. Hughes comments that meekness and gentleness are not incompatible with sternness, and that Paul had shown sternness in his letter to the Galatians.[7] Guthrie entitles vv. 1–2 as "Meekness Not Weakness."[8]

The personal beginning "I myself, Paul" emphasizes that he is giving a personal defense to the accusations made by his opponents. But Plummer may go too far when he asserts that "I, Paul" is primarily "an assertion of his authority," and that he is "perhaps somewhat scornful."[9] Witherington and Sampley are probably nearer the mark when they compare Greco-Roman rhetoric of the era especially on self-praise.[10] Better still, E. A. Judge comments, "Paul found himself a reluctant and unwelcomed competitor in the field of professional sophistry and . . . he promoted a deliberate collision with its standards of value."[11] This opens up the possibility that Paul might well be using parody among those who knew the conventions of this style of rhetoric. Barrett comments, "It is very probable that he (Paul) echoes the language of his opponents."[12]

The alleged contrast between Paul's supposed weakness when he was present and supposed boldness when he wrote by letter from a distance derives some support from 1 Cor 2:3–5, where he acknowledges that he came to Corinth in much fear and with trembling. Paul's preaching reflected the message of the cross. His way of preaching embodied this.

On vv. 2–3, Barrett emphatically argues that "according to the flesh" (NRSV, "according to human standards") meant something very different

---

6. Bjerkelund, *Parakalō*, 24–58 and 190; cf. Danker, BDAG, 764–65.
7. Hughes, *Second Corinthians*, 345–46.
8. Guthrie, *2 Corinthians*, 466.
9. Plummer, *Second Corinthians*, 272.
10. Witherington, *Conflict and Community in Corinth*, 433; Sampley, "Paul, His Opponents in 2 Corinthians 10–13, and the Rhetorical Handbooks."
11. Judge, "Paul's Boasting in Relation to Contemporary Professional Practice," 47.
12. Barrett, *Second Corinthians*, 247.

in Paul than it did to his opponents.[13] "I ask" (v. 2), Plummer suggests, takes up and repeats "appeal" or "beseech" in a lower key.[14] Thrall helpfully renders vv. 3–4a, "For though we live in the human world, we do not campaign in merely human ways; for the weapons of our warfare are not merely human, but powerful for God, to destroy strongholds."

Windisch regards it as a part of Paul's rhetorical strategy to begin this first section with a moderate tone before taking a sharper response to his opponents.[15] Most writers have followed him, e.g., Witherington.[16] Tasker expresses Paul's dilemma well: "Paul regards it as axiomatic that a true minister of Christ should always use gentle methods in seeking to win submission of men to the Saviour, and that they should employ more severe methods only as a last resort."[17] "To be bold" is to act with decision and courage; to exhibit the character which the opponents of the apostle said he assumed only when absent.[18] "Acting according to human standards" means with undue authoritarianism. If some of these opponents were of the "gnostic" kind, they may well have accused him of lacking "spiritual" gifts by substituting rhetoric for charismatic gifts.[19] Thrall lists seven types of possible accusation against him.

Paul allows that we live in the flesh (Greek) *en sarki* in vv. 2–3. But this, as Barrett pointed out, does not mean "in the flesh" in the sense discussed in Rom 8:8, where it denotes all that is worldly, godless, and limiting.[20] In this passage, "*in* the flesh" means simply living an ordinary earthly life, or being human; while "*according to* the flesh" (Greek, *kata sarka*) means living according to our worldly and self-centered nature. Paul plays on the Greek *en sarka* and *kata sarka*, as Martin says.[21] J. B. Phillips renders this as "Although of course we lead normal human lives, the battle we are fighting is on the spiritual level."[22]

---

13. Barrett, *Second Corinthians*, 249.
14. Plummer, *Second Corinthians*, 274.
15. Windisch, *Der zweite Korintherbrief*, 292.
16. Witherington, *Conflict and Community in Corinth*, 434–41.
17. Tasker, *The Second Epistle of Paul to the Corinthians*, 132–33.
18. Hodge, *The Second Epistle to the Corinthians*, 231.
19. Thrall, *Second Corinthians*, 605.
20. Furnish, *II Corinthians*, 457.
21. Martin, *Second Corinthians*, 300.
22. Phillips, *Letters to Young Churches*, 81.

PART II: EXEGESIS

This leads on to Paul's use of analogy based on military activity in vv. 3–6. He speaks of his labor in warfare terms: "we wage war" (Greek, *strateuometha*, v. 3, and *strateias* in v. 4), "weapons" (Greek, *hopla*), "to destroy strongholds" (Greek, *ochurōmatōn*), and "we take captives" (*aichmalōtizontes*, in v. 5).[23] As Gale points out, Paul uses military metaphors elsewhere, e.g., in 2 Cor 6:7; Rom 7:23; 13:12-13; and 1 Thess 5:8. He could also have cited 1 Cor 9:7; 1 Tim 1:18; 6:12; and 2 Tim 2:3-4. Paul's "weapons" are called negatively "not merely human," and, positively, "powerful" (Greek, *dynata*), with which we may compare Eph 6:12-14, also on spiritual warfare, where "human" is weak, and the Spirit is power. Robinson has convincingly argued this.[24] "Not merely human" means not relying on eloquence, rhetoric, or a powerful personality. Chrysostom lists these "merely human" things as "wealth, glory, power, loquaciousness, cleverness, half-truths, flatteries, hypocrisies, whatever is similar to these."[25] The "spiritual" means "for God" in the power of the Holy Spirit. Hughes calls these weapons "divinely powerful."[26] In this instance, the false apostles or Paul's opponents are specifically cited as the enemies against whom Paul is fighting.

The language in v. 6 becomes even stronger. The Greek *ekdikēsai* is rendered "to punish" in NRSV, although Danker translates *ekdikeō* as "to procure justice for someone" in general, but especially "to punish" or "to inflict an appropriate penalty for wrong done" in 2 Cor 10:6.[27] How does this square with "the meekness and gentleness of Christ" (v. 1)? The "false apostles" to whom Paul is referring were deceivers and newcomers to the church in Corinth who were undermining Paul's work. In v. 5, they were "a proud obstacle to the knowledge of God" (Greek, *hypsōma epairomenon*), like a raised rampart.[28] Hence, in v. 6 Paul prepares to take stern and firm measures. Paul Barnett writes, "We do well to follow Paul in his realistic estimate of the entrenched power of unbelief and pride in the human mind. Only the right weapons will subdue and capture this proud fortified rebel who places himself over God."[29] Paul proclaims that "walls must be torn

23. Gale, *The Use of Analogy in the Letters of Paul*, 163–64.
24. Robinson, *The Body*, 20.
25 325 Chrysostom, "Homilies on the Second Epistle to the Corinthians," Homily 21, 376.
26. Hughes, *Second Corinthians*, 350–51.
27. Danker, BDAG, 300–301.
28. Kruse, *The Second Epistle of Paul to the* Corinthians, 174.
29. Barnet, *The Message of 2 Corinthians*, 158–59.

down," ramparts overcome, and enemy soldiers captured.[30] He follows through his military metaphor. He even takes captive for Christ "every thought" (v. 5b), to ensure that "your obedience is complete" (v. 6).

Furnish begins the next section with a vivid translation of v. 7: "Look at what is staring you in the face" (NRSV, "Look at what is before your eyes"; NEB, "Look facts in the face").[31] Hughes comments, "If they would but look into their hearts and face the irrefutable facts of their spiritual experience, they would perforce have to acknowledge that Paul was in truth their own genuine apostle and reject the unsubstantial claims of those spurious apostles who intruded themselves into their community."[32] Some, however, have taken the sentence as a question, which is grammatically possible.[33] In this case, "the facts" (Greek, *ta kata prosopon*) can be interpreted to mean "the outward appearance" (as AV/KJV and RV margin) or "what can be seen outwardly" (Bultmann).[34] Guthrie links this with those who are looking at things as they appear on the surface.[35]

Verses 7b–11 explore further Paul's claim to authority. In v. 7b, he calls for a consideration of his relationship to Christ: "As you belong to Christ, so also do we." Nevertheless, Thrall points out that he is defending his authority, not his Christian faith. She further argues that Paul may be alluding to the "Christ group" of 1 Cor 1:12 ("I belong to Christ").[36] Second, in v. 8 he underlines that he will not be ashamed of boasting about his position of authority, which the Lord gave for building them up, not for tearing them down.

Third, in v. 9, Paul does not wish to seem as though he was trying to frighten them with his letters. The thought may seem obscure because Paul chooses to follow a fine line between rebuke and more gentle care and concern, as he attempted earlier. Even Thrall acknowledges that Paul's line of thought becomes obscure.[37] Verse 9, she says, has the force of an imperative. She suggests: "Let me not seem, as it were to scare you by my letters."[38]

---

30. Guthrie, *2 Corinthians*, 474-75.
31. Furnish, *II Corinthians*, 686.
32. Hughes, *Second Corinthians*, 355.
33. Bultmann, *Second Corinthians*, 187.
34. Cf. Harris, *Second Corinthians*, 686-88.
35. Guthrie, *2 Corinthians*, 477.
36. Thrall offers six interpretations of this complex verse; cf. Thrall, *2 Corinthians*, 620-23.
37. Thrall, *2 Corinthians*, 626.
38. Thrall, *2 Corinthians*, 627.

Furnish suggests, "lest I should seem to be scaring you with my letters."[39] This is many pastors' dilemma: how to exercise genuine authority without appearing to be unduly authoritarian. If the opponents claimed that they were "of Christ," this is only the cry of 1 Cor 1:12, unless we understand a different interpretation of this verse.[40]

In v. 10, Paul addresses what his opponents claim, namely that his letters may seem strong and effective, but his personal presence does not live up to this. Paul appears to be responding to a criticism that is current in Corinth. Guthrie comments, "Paul does not want to be perceived as terrorizing his congregation through his letters."[41] The claim that Paul's letters are weighty and "strong" (Greek, *ischyros*) or "forceful" (NIV) may mean "violent" or "impressive."[42] But his opponents in Corinth claimed that in his physical presence he was "weak" (Greek, *asthenēs*) and in speech "contemptible" (*exouthenēmenos*), i.e., his oratory supposedly had no merit, and was worthy of disdain. In v. 11, Paul concludes that when he is present, he will act in accordance with his letters. Guthrie paraphrases: "There will be an absolute correspondence between the words he has written and the actions he will take. . . . Paul's authority does not consist of mere words."[43]

Questions for reflection

1. Do we find that we can combine firmness (when it is needed) with "the meekness and gentleness of Christ"? Does Christ's meekness and gentleness become a false alibi for being insufficiently firm? On which side of the fine line are we more tempted to fall? Can we firmly "appeal" without command?

2. Do we find it easier to write a letter from a distance than talking face to face? Or is the balance in the reverse direction? Are both sometimes needed?

3. As Christians, are we sufficiently aware that we live as ordinary people in the world? Does idealism sometimes take the place of realism?

---

39. Furnish, *II Corinthians*, 465.
40. Cf. Thiselton, *First Epistle to the Corinthians*, 121–31.
41. Guthrie, *2 Corinthians*, 482.
42. Danker, BDAG, 483–84.
43. Guthrie, *2 Corinthians*, 483–84.

2. Paul and his rivals: proper and improper boasting (10:12–18)

¹² We do not dare to classify or compare ourselves with some of those who commend themselves. But when they measure themselves by one another, and compare themselves with one another, they do not show good sense. ¹³ We, however, will not boast beyond limits, but will keep within the field that God has assigned to us, to reach out even as far as you. ¹⁴ For we were not overstepping our limits when we reached you; we were the first to come all the way to you with the good news of Christ. ¹⁵ We do not boast beyond limits, that is, in the labors of others; but our hope is that, as your faith increases, our sphere of action among you may be greatly enlarged, ¹⁶ so that we may proclaim the good news in lands beyond you, without boasting of work already done in someone else's sphere of action. ¹⁷ "Let the one who boasts, boast in the Lord." ¹⁸ For it is not those who commend themselves that are approved, but those whom the Lord commends.

J. B. Phillips' rendering of the Greek is perhaps more helpful on passages in 2 Corinthians than in most other books. On v. 12, he reveals Paul's use of irony or sarcasm well: "Of course we shouldn't dare include ourselves in the same class as those who write their own testimonials, or even to compare ourselves with them!" Paul explains his position in four steps. In v. 12, he rejects the wrong kind of comparisons between human leaders or personalities such as bedeviled the boasting of 1 Cor 1:12: "I belong to Paul" or "I belong to Apollos," or "I belong to Cephas," or "I belong to Christ." (We may note that David Hall, following Chrysostom, contends that these are fictitious names for opponents whom Paul wishes to keep anonymous.)[44] Paul is emphatic that his "boasting" is quite different from the boasting of his opponents.

In vv. 13–15a, he affirms that he must not overstep the bounds of ministry by making wild claims: he must not "boast beyond limits." The NRSV repeats "beyond limits" three times. In vv. 15b–16, he expresses the hope of extending his mission "in lands beyond you." Finally, in vv. 17–18, he explains that the only ground of boasting is the Lord, and whom the Lord commends. Phillips renders the verse: "It is not self-commendation that matters, it is winning the approval of God."[45]

---

44. Hall, *The Unity of the Corinthian Correspondence*, 5–8.
45. Phillips, *Letters to Young Churches*, 83.

In v. 12, there is a textual variant concerning "We do not dare to rank ourselves or compare ourselves with those who commend themselves. On the contrary, they lack understanding, measuring themselves with themselves...." In other words, the shorter reading omits the Greek *ou syniasin* (*[they] do not understand*). Paul himself is seen as measuring and comparing himself with a true apostle. The longer reading regards Paul's opponents as doing the measuring and comparison. Metzger, Thrall, and others evaluate the validity of each reading carefully.[46]

Metzger concludes that the shorter text, which is mainly in witnesses of the Western text (D*, G, it[d, g, ar], Ambrosiaster) "is doubtless the result of an accident in transcription, when the eye of a copyist passed from [Greek] *ou* to *ouk* and omitted the intervening words."[47] The United Bible Society Committee followed the reading of $\mathfrak{p}^{46}$, ℵ, B, 33, and other MSS. Thrall adds, "Paul's conviction that he is validated by the Lord is one of 'the facts of the case.'"[48] His opponents, by contrast, commend themselves. Self-commendation is not always wrong, but "drifts into unhealthy attitudes and behaviors."[49] Paul's opponents boast of what they have to offer. Paul's "But" (v. 12) marks the difference. The Greek *metreō* can mean *measure* but is better translated as evaluate.[50] To compare one's ministry in the light of others is called "clueless" by Guthrie.[51]

In vv. 13–15a, Paul insists that *his* concept of ministry is not beyond bounds. The key terms in Greek are *ouk eis ta ametra* (NRSV, "not beyond limits") and *kata to metron tou kanonos hou emerisen hēmin ho Theos* ("according to the measure [NRSV, 'keep within the field'] that God has assigned to us"). In other words, Paul's opponents were boasting beyond all reasonable bounds; but Paul refuses to go beyond what God assigned to him. The cardinal mistake of the false "apostles" was to measure themselves by other human leaders. Paul "boasts" within the boundaries of the assignment that God has given him. Furnish extends the meaning of Greek *kanōn* to denote *jurisdiction*.[52]

---

46. Metzger, *A Textual Commentary*, 514; Thrall, *Second Corinthians*, 636–40.
47. Metzger, *A Textual Commentary*, 514.
48. Thrall, *Second Corinthians*, 636.
49. Guthrie, *2 Corinthians*, 489.
50. Danker, BDAG, 643.
51. Guthrie, *2 Corinthians*, 490.
52. Furnish, *II Corinthians*, 465.

As Thrall comments, "Paul here [i.e., in v. 14] substantiates the claim which emerges implicitly from v. 13, i.e., that he will not exceed the acceptable limit when he includes Corinth in the area of apostolic achievements he can boast about."[53] With several other commentators, she takes the Greek verb *ephthasamen* to mean "we arrived first" (v. 14b). In other words, he has not trespassed on another person's territory. Some might suggest that this view of legitimate "territories" anticipates later notions of "parishes" in which outreach is especially legitimate. Paul had founded the church in Corinth. Where did the opponents come from? Paul had spent eighteen months of hard work (Greek, *kopos*) in Corinth. 2 Corinthians 11:27 speaks of "toil and hardship."

Paul then expresses the hope of extending (Greek, *megalynthēnai*) the mission in vv. 15b-16.[54] In Rom 15:14, 18, he hopes to extend his mission to Spain, on which Robert Jewett has some extensive and relevant linguistic, cultural, and other comments.[55] In geographical terms Paul's mission spreads from East to West.

Finally, Paul concludes this chapter by repeating the words of 1 Cor 1:31, "Let the one who boasts, boast in the Lord," which is a reformulation of Jer 9:23 (LXX).[56] Karl Barth magnificently expounds 1 Cor 1:31 in his book *The Resurrection of the Dead*. He writes, "The main defect of Corinthian conditions . . . Paul sees to consist in the boldness, assurance, and enthusiasm with which they believe, not in God, but in their own belief in God and in particular leaders and heroes; in the fact that they confuse belief with specific human experiences, convictions, trends of thought and theories." Barth continues, "Against this, the clarion call of Paul rings out: 'Let no man glory in men' (3:21), or expressed in positive form: 'He that glorieth, let him glory in the Lord' (1:31 [and 2 Cor 10:17])."[57] In 1 Corinthians, he says, this "of God" is "clearly the secret nerve of this whole . . . section."[58] This certainly applies to 2 Corinthians, where the newcomers found a ready response to the same ideas. This also reflects the spirit of the passage in Jeremiah, where the theme is "I am the LORD." It is a fitting conclusion to a discussion of "boasting." There was a tradition of Greek

---

53. Thrall, *Second Corinthians*, 648.
54. Danker, BDAG, 623.
55. Jewett, *Romans*, 74-91.
56. Thrall, *Second Corinthians*, 652.
57. Barth, *The Resurrection of the Dead*, 17.
58. Barth, *The Resurrection of the Dead*, 18; cf. 19-21.

heroes boasting in qualities that characterized them: Odysseus in his cunning, Achilles in his strength, and so on. The Christian, Paul says, should rather boast in the Lord.

The final verse (v. 18) clinches the matter: only the person whom the Lord commends has passed, as it were, the test. Guthrie comments, "His (Paul's) 'self' commendation is thoroughly God-centered."[59]

Questions for reflection

1. Do we sometimes try to evaluate our progress (or lack of it) by comparing ourselves with other people?
2. As long as it is by God's direction, do we too easily limit what God requires of us, or do we look for moving "beyond"?

3. Paul uses "the speech of the fool": to which Christ did he pledge the Corinthians? (11:1–4)

> I wish you would bear with me in a little foolishness. Do bear with me! ² I feel a divine jealousy for you, for I promised you in marriage to one husband, to present you as a chaste virgin to Christ. ³ But I am afraid that as the serpent deceived Eve by its cunning, your thoughts will be led astray from a sincere and pure devotion to Christ. ⁴ For if anyone comes preaching any other Jesus than the one we have preached, or if you receive a different Spirit from the one you did receive, or a different gospel from the one you received, you put up with it well enough. (11:4 author's translation.)

It is important to note three key facts. First, in chapter 11, that Paul not only uses irony, but that he also adopts "the speech of the fool" in accordance with accepted rhetorical practices. Several major studies underline this. One such study is L. L. Welborn, *Paul, the Fool of Christ*, although Welborn bases his approach mainly on 1 Cor 1–4.[60] In 1 Cor 4, Paul ironically portrays the apostles as gladiators struggling in the arena while some of the Corinthians lounge at ease in armchairs and applaud. It is Paul's ironic critique of their false triumphalism.[61] Without us, he says in deep irony,

---

59. Guthrie, *2 Corinthians*, 499.
60. Welborn, *Paul, the Fool of Christ*.
61. Thiselton, *The First Epistle to the Corinthians*, 344–65.

you reign as kings (v. 8) and are rich and glutted with food, as he unfolds the metaphor of a great pageant in which they look down on the humble apostles. Welborn relates this to the humiliated Christ in 1 Cor 1:18 (the message of the cross as foolishness) and elsewhere.

The second key point to note is that the Christ of the false apostles is "another Jesus" revealed through "another Spirit" (11: 3, 4). He is not the Christ to whom Paul betrothed them. The most decisive modern work here is David R. Hall, *The Unity of the Corinthian Correspondence*. As Hall points out, this is not "Jesus Christ and him crucified!" (1 Cor 1:17, 18; 2:1-9).[62] He adds, "In 2 Corinthians the connection between the suffering of Christ and the sufferings of the apostles becomes even more prominent. Paul describes his near-death experience in 1:3-11 and comments: 'as the sufferings of Christ abound to us, so also through Christ our encouragement abounds' (v. 5)."[63]

Just as important, Hall comments, "In both 1 and 2 Corinthians a contrast is drawn between two gospels and two lifestyles. Central to Paul's gospel was the crucifixion of Jesus. . . . Paul's opponents, by contrast, boasted of their strength."[64] They were inspired by "a different Spirit."[65] Paul's opponents taught "a different Jesus and a different gospel."[66]

It is no wonder that Paul uses such strong language in chapter 11. This brings us to a third point. Paul does use such strong language elsewhere when the identity of Jesus and the gospel are at stake. In Phil 3:2-7, he writes, "Beware of dogs, beware of evil workers, beware of those who mutilate the flesh. . . . Yet whatever gains I had, these I have come to regard as loss because of Christ." Notoriously in Galatians he accuses some of them as turning to "a different gospel" (Gal 1:6). He says that even if an angel proclaimed another gospel, "let that one be accursed" (v. 8). Galatians is no less "violent" than 2 Corinthians 11. As Hall repeatedly argues, it is strange why so many in the 1980s and 1990s made such a special case out of this chapter as to propose that it constituted a separate letter. We should regard theories that break 2 Corinthians into separate letters with caution.

In v. 1, the words "bear with me" (repeated in v. 4) are clearly ironic. By contrast, the Corinthians bear well with (or tolerate) those who proclaim

---

62. Hall, *The Unity of the Corinthian Correspondence*, 154.
63. Hall, *The Unity of the Corinthian Correspondence*, 155.
64. Hall, *The Unity of the Corinthian Correspondence*, 163.
65. Hall, *The Unity of the Corinthian Correspondence*, 170.
66. Hall, *The Unity of the Corinthian Correspondence*, 154.

another Jesus! In vv. 2–3, Paul states his godly jealousy over their choosing to be betrothed to another Jesus, which would be spiritually adulterous. The preposition "for" (Greek, *gar*, not translated in the NRSV) is important because Paul is explaining why he is urgent about the Corinthians bearing with him. He is jealous about their doctrinal purity (vv. 2–3), and they have already tolerated and listened to dangerous false apostles (v. 4). The word "jealous" (Greek, *zēlō*) is used positively, not in the negative sense. Thrall speaks of "a jealous concern inspired by God, or God-like jealousy."[67] God describes himself as a "jealous God" (Exod 20:5). Paul is jealous about the Corinthians being seduced away from the true Jesus to "another Jesus." He uses betrothal language drawn from the Old Testament (Isa 54:5–6; 62:5; Jer 3:14; Hos 2:19–20). Thrall includes Excursus IX on "Another Jesus, Spirit, and gospel."[68] We have already noted Hall's comments. False apostles seduce some Corinthians to spiritual adultery.

The betrothal tradition in which it was the privilege of the father to present the bride stems from firm biblical roots. Hughes comments, "It is the father's right to give his daughter in marriage to an approved bridegroom."[69] Paul speaks of himself as their spiritual father elsewhere (1 Cor 4:15). Impostors are trying to seduce them away from purity and faithfulness. The danger of seduction prompts Paul to cite the analogy of Eden and the serpent (v. 3). The episode in Eden brought havoc by cunning and trickery (Greek, *panourgia*). Paul seeks to guard them from "being ruined" (Greek, *phtharē*). On v. 4, Harris notes that the triad Jesus-Spirit-gospel provides a summary of the Christian faith.[70] Guthrie notes, "The real Jesus, the Spirit, and the gospel are inseparably linked."[71] The false "gospel" was based on a wrong identification of Jesus Christ and the Holy Spirit. Too much is at stake for Paul to show tolerance to the false teachers.

Questions for reflection

1. Can the virtue of tolerance ever be stretched too far? Does this depend on what is at stake?

---

67. Thrall, *2 Corinthians*, 660.
68. Thrall, *2 Corinthians*, 667–71.
69. Hughes, *Second Corinthians*, 374.
70. Harris, *Second Corinthians*, 744.
71. Guthrie, *2 Corinthians*, 510.

2. How does "godly jealousy" differ from jealousy in other contexts? When is jealousy legitimate or even necessary?

3. Does the speech of "the fool" reflect parts of 1 Corinthians?

4. The "foolish" speech continues: Paul and the "super-apostles" (11:5-15)

⁵ I think that I am not in the least inferior to these super-apostles. ⁶ I may be untrained in speech, but not in knowledge; certainly in every way and in all things we have made this evident to you.

⁷ Did I commit a sin by humbling myself so that you might be exalted, because I proclaimed God's good news to you free of charge? ⁸ I robbed other churches by accepting support from them in order to serve you. ⁹ And when I was with you and was in need, I did not burden anyone, for my needs were supplied by the friends who came from Macedonia. So I refrained and will continue to refrain from burdening you in any way. ¹⁰ As the truth of Christ is in me, this boast of mine will not be silenced in the regions of Achaia. ¹¹ And why? Because I do not love you? God knows I do!

¹² And what I do I will also continue to do, in order to deny an opportunity to those who want an opportunity to be recognized as our equals in what they boast about. ¹³ For such boasters are false apostles, deceitful workers, disguising themselves as apostles of Christ. ¹⁴ And no wonder! Even Satan disguises himself as an angel of light. ¹⁵ So it is not strange if his ministers also disguise themselves as ministers of righteousness. Their end will match their deeds.

The false apostles levelled two accusations against Paul. First, he is an inferior public speaker in rhetoric. Second, he preaches free of charge, and does not claim a fee like professional orators. In v. 5, Paul denies the first charge because he is concerned with the *content* of the gospel, not with style, form, or rhetoric. In v. 6, he contrasts speech or rhetoric with knowledge of God. Then in v. 7 he comes to the second charge. He calls the false apostles "super-apostles" in v. 5 with heavy irony (Greek, *hyperlian*; not found in Greek earlier than Paul, and literally meaning "over" or "very much"). The word shows the arrogance of Paul's opponents, and how much they disparage him by comparison. They claim superiority in rhetoric, in contrast to Paul's concern for revelation, knowledge, and truth. Paul's awareness of his inadequacy as a rhetorician is reflected in 1 Cor 2:1-4, which recalls his initial arrival in Corinth. As Barnett reminds us, rhetoric was a long-established, highly esteemed profession in Greco-Roman cities, for which Apollos was highly respected.[72] Paul readily accepted that in person he was unimpressive (10:10). But this is not to say that he was a poor speaker. He is focusing on a limited comparison with his new opponents.

These newcomers wish that Paul had charged a professional fee since this would seem to place him on a comparable footing to them. Paul asks ironically, "Did I sin in bringing the gospel to Corinth free of charge?" (vv. 7). In v. 13, Paul calls them "false apostles, deceitful workers, disguising themselves as apostles of Christ." He adds in v. 14 that Satan, too, disguises himself as an angel of light." These false apostles were opportunists, seeking any opportunity to present their ministry as equal to Paul's.

The aggressive claims of his opponents about pay make Paul more than ever determined to continue to preach the gospel free of charge (v. 12). The phrase "ministers of righteousness" in v. 15 could be an allusion to their stricter understanding of the Jewish law. The reference to the churches of Macedonia in v. 9 (including Philippi) shows that Paul was humble enough to accept support (Greek, *opsōnion*) as long as it was a gift and a sharing in the gospel (Phil 4:15-17). Martin and Barnett stress that those who labored with their hands and were of allegedly lower social status contributed in contrast to the so-called professionals of generally wealthy Corinth.[73] It was because of the Macedonian churches that Paul could free the Corinthians from the "burden" (v. 9) of meeting his financial needs. "Burden" (Greek, *katamanarkaō*) was used specially of relations of dependence between patrons and clients, e.g., obligations of various kinds.[74] Harris suggests that Paul brought with him to Corinth financial or other resources from Macedonia, as he had earlier been partnered with Priscilla and Aquila (1 Cor 4:11-12).[75] Nevertheless, elsewhere Paul has insisted that normally permanent teachers in the church should be paid (1 Cor 9:3-14; Gal 6:6; 1 Tim 5:17-18).[76]

Attitudes to boasting are quite different in modern Western cultures from those of ancient Greco-Roman cultures. In the modern West, partly

---

72. Barnett, *Second Corinthians*, 509.
73. Martin, *2 Corinthians*, 344-45; Barnett, *Second Corinthians*, 513.
74. Keener, *1-2 Corinthians*, 229.
75. Harris, *Second Corinthians*, 761-62.
76. Barnett, *Second Corinthians*, 518; Thrall, *2 Corinthians*, 699-708.

due to Christian influence, humility and self-effacement have traditionally been regarded as virtues. As Barnett points out, "People in Greek or Roman antiquity possessed no hope of glory in an after-life. A detached immortality was most one could expect. Therefore it was customary to achieve 'glory' in this life, and to boast of one's achievements in this life."[77] In our discussion of 3:1–6, we considered the monument erected by Babbius, still standing at the west side of the *Agora* in Corinth today, which inscribes in stone, "Babbius erected this monument at his own expense." We noted that he officially approved the monument as "duovir" (a high official in Roman Corinth).[78] This is a universally agreed example of self-promotion. We also cited the pavement left by Erastus together with his title, which still can be seen on the site of ancient Corinth.

Betz attempts to draw a fine distinction between philosophers and rhetoricians in Paul's day. Socrates, as portrayed by Plato, represents the philosophers who denounced the rhetorical techniques of the Sophists, who indeed charged fees, and philosophers who insisted that the pursuit of knowledge in philosophy required no payment whatever. Thrall, however, argues that since the time of Plato this distinction became less clear-cut and prominent, and that it is unlikely that Paul is consciously reflecting this earlier controversy.[79]

Questions for reflection

1. Could we be seduced into evaluating particular ministries only in terms of certain qualities that we have selected? Might we ever consider rhetorical skills to be more important than the content of the gospel?
2. Do we help to ensure that our ordained ministers, pastors, or teachers are regularly maintained financially?
3. How might we be tempted to boast either of our strengths or our weaknesses? What do we think of Paul's inversion of "boasting"?

---

77. Barnett, *The Message of 2 Corinthians*, 173.
78. Thiselton, *First Epistle*, 8–9; Thiselton, *1 Corinthians*, 22.
79. Thrall, *2 Corinthians*, 679–81; Guthrie, *The Sophists*.

PART II: EXEGESIS

5. Paul boasts about his sufferings (11:16–33)

[16] I repeat, let no one think that I am a fool; but if you do, then accept me as a fool, so that I too may boast a little. [17] What I am saying in regard to this boastful confidence, I am saying not with the Lord's authority, but as a fool; [18] since many boast according to human standards, I will also boast. [19] For you gladly put up with fools, being wise yourselves! [20] For you put up with it when someone makes slaves of you, or preys upon you, or takes advantage of you, or puts on airs, or gives you a slap in the face. [21] To my shame, I must say, we were too weak for that!

But whatever anyone dares to boast of—I am speaking as a fool—I also dare to boast of that. [22] Are they Hebrews? So am I. Are they Israelites? So am I. Are they descendants of Abraham? So am I. [23] Are they ministers of Christ? I am talking like a madman—I am a better one: with far greater labors, far more imprisonments, with countless floggings, and often near death. [24] Five times I have received from the Jews the forty lashes minus one. [25] Three times I was thrashed with a birching, once I was stoned, three times I was shipwrecked; for a night and a day I was adrift at sea. (11:25 author's translation.) [26] on frequent journeys, in danger from rivers, danger from bandits, danger from my own people, danger from Gentiles, danger in the city, danger in the wilderness, danger at sea, danger from false brothers and sisters; [27] in toil and hardship, through many a sleepless night, hungry and thirsty, often without food, cold and naked. [28] And, besides other things, I am under daily pressure because of my anxiety for all the churches. [29] Who is weak, and I am not weak? Who is made to stumble, and I am not indignant?

[30] If I must boast, I will boast of the things that show my weakness. [31] The God and Father of the Lord Jesus (blessed be he forever!) knows that I do not lie. [32] In Damascus, the governor under King Aretas guarded the city of Damascus in order to seize me, [33] but I was let down in a basket through a window in the wall, and escaped from his hands.

In vv. 16–21, Paul repeats his general appeal for the false apostles to understand why he deliberately subverts their boasting. In vv. 21b–22 he "boasts" of genuine authentic marks of apostleship, for example his Jewish pedigree. But in vv. 23–33 he "boasts" of his trials and weakness. He highlights matters of difficulty and hardship: hard work, imprisonment, floggings, and threats to his life. He is again ironically inverting the ancient convention of boasting.

This reaches its grand climax in vv. 32–33. It was well-known in the ancient Greco-Roman world that special commendation was given to the brave soldier or mercenary who was literally "first over the wall," when a city was besieged. Imagine how the besieged defenders would pour molten lead and whatever was to hand on the head of any soldier rash enough to climb rickety ladders up the wall of the city. Paul, with supreme irony, does not directly use the phrase "first over the wall," but people would see the allusion: he points out that his travel "over the wall" was in the opposite direction: he was escaping from King Aretas (v. 32) in order to escape opposition from enemies in Damascus! He was indeed "first over the wall," but *in the opposite direction*! This is a clear example of an outstanding Pauline "joke." Many scholars, including E. A. Judge and Stephen Travis, have since made the point very clear.[80] It may look like boasting even in a cowardly escape!

On Paul's clams to be utterly rooted in his Jewish origins, Barnett comments, "Not to have been a Jewish apostle would in the nature of things have been a fatal defect in one who claimed to represent the Messiah Jesus."[81] Hence, in v. 22, Paul asserts, "Are they Hebrews? So am I. Are they Israelites? So am I. Are they descendants of Abraham? So am I." Paul proves his equality with rival missionaries. He is their equal with respect to race and ancestry. But he is incomparably effective as an agent of Christ.[82] "Hebrews" may denote those who were born Jews, in contrast to proselytes, or it may denote a pure-blooded Jew, or possibly a Jew who can speak Aramaic, or a Jew with close family ties with the Holy Land. The reference to Abraham recalls God's covenant promises. Now from v. 23 he recounts his greater missionary endeavors. In Thrall's words, "He has endured many more potentially fatal dangers."[83]

Barrett argues that in vv. 23–30 Paul is comparing himself not with the false apostles but with the Jerusalem apostles. But most commentators reject this, arguing that Paul has too recently addressed the problem of the false apostles in vv. 19–23. Guthrie states that in v. 20 Paul describes their conduct as "slapping the Corinthians in the face" (NRSV; Greek, *eis prosopon humas*

---

80. Windisch, *Der zweite Korintherbrief*, 364; Travis, "Paul's Boasting in 2 Corinthians"; Martin, *2 Corinthians*, 384–85.
81. Barnett, *The Message of 2 Corinthians*, 173.
82. Thrall, *2 Corinthians*, 722.
83. Thrall, *2 Corinthians*, 722.

PART II: EXEGESIS

derei).[84] Nevertheless Barrett comments, "to accept the Judaizers' 'Gospel' is to fall back into the bondage of heathenism."[85]

In v. 20, Paul's word "slap" can also mean "to beat," as in "beat you in the face." No wonder that he is deeply jealous for his converts! In 11:23 and 27, he lists the many difficulties of his work, including imprisonments, beatings, staring death in the face, exhausting work and hard labor, often going without sleep, suffering hunger and thirst, doing without food, and facing cold temperatures when he is without adequate clothing. In 6:4–10, he has already mentioned the experiences of being put in jail, enduring beatings, sleepless nights, and feeling as if he was dying. Guthrie comments, "The combination of ancient travel in a variety of both rural and urban contexts, supporting himself through manual labour as a tent maker, battling opponents, and overseeing a variety of fledgling churches across the Mediterranean world—all of this would have made his work onerous at times."[86] He adds that the strain of cross-cultural ministry, theological training of converts, evangelistic proclamation, and conflict would have greatly added to all this. Paul's work as a missionary pastor extended far beyond his work in Corinth, as Furnish reminds us.[87]

In vv. 24–25, Paul enumerates specific trials. He lists that on five occasions he received thirty-nine lashes from Jewish leaders; three times he was beaten with birch rods; once he was pummeled with stones; three times he was shipwrecked; a night and for a day he had been adrift in the open sea. The thirty-nine lashes were from *Jewish synagogue officials*. This was administered with a strap of three hide thongs. Paul repeatedly faced this punishment. In spite of this, Paul usually began a visit to a new town by preaching in the synagogue. This shows how courageous he was. On three occasions (v. 24) he suffered the *Roman* punishment of a beating with birch rods (Greek, *errabdisēn*). Acts 16:23 recounts how Paul and Silas were "beaten with rods" by the Roman magistrates at Philippi. Stonings constituted a Jewish punishment for apostasy or blasphemy (Lev 20:2; 24:14; Deut 17:5–7), recounted in Acts 14:19–20. Shipwrecks (Greek, *enauagēsa*) were suffered three times, together with spending a night and a day adrift in the open sea. Vessels did not carry lifeboats. Sea

---

84. Guthrie, *2 Corinthians*, 541.
85. Barrett, *Second Corinthians*, 291.
86. Guthrie, *2 Corinthians*, 554.
87. Furnish, *II Corinthians*, 515.

voyages were usually limited to the months between May and October, because of dangerous winter weather.

In v. 26, Paul recounts a series of "dangers," i.e., life-threatening situations. These occurred often during his travels. He uses a grammatical form that indicates "the varied abundance of evidence on the topic."[88] His use of "in" denotes various contexts. These include, for example (v. 26), dangers from rivers, dangers from bandits, dangers from his own people, dangers from gentiles, dangers in the city, dangers in the wilderness, dangers at sea, and dangers among false brothers. Harris notes that the Taurus Mountains, between Perga and Pisidian Antioch were notorious for cascading rivers as well as bandits.[89]

In v. 27, Paul gives a general characterization of his trials. They include exhausting work and hard labor (the Greek words imply fatigue and exhaustion), often going without sleep, hunger and thirst, and cold temperatures with inadequate clothing. It is too easy to glide past these verses. But finally, in vv. 28–29, Paul reaches his climax: his pressure of anxiety about all of the Pauline churches. This includes the emotional strain or "weight" of such God-given responsibility. This weighs on him every day. No wonder his reaction to the false apostles is so fierce! He asks in v. 29: "Who is made to stumble, and I am not indignant?" (i.e., towards those who have caused him to stumble). Barnett contrasts those who imagine that church-leadership and Christian ministry can become an "ego-trip" with Paul's very different concept of ministry.[90]

We have already explained above how vv. 30–33 constitute the climax of Paul speech in the form of ironic humor. He had been first over the wall—but in the opposite direction! His "weakness" is to reflect the crucified Christ. His "power" is in weakness.

Questions for reflection

1. Do we genuinely view sharing Christ's "weakness" as a sign of authenticity and power?
2. Do we think of power in ministry as triumphalist, authoritarian, and a way of impressing others?

---

88. Guthrie, *2 Corinthians*, 559.
89. Harris, *Second Corinthians*, 806.
90. Barnett, *The Message of 2 Corinthians*, 175.

3. Do we regard tolerance as a universal virtue to be shown in any and every context?
4. Do we consider the Old Testament as part of our authenticity or as a source of embarrassment?
5. How do minor sacrifices (in some parts of the world) compare with Paul's very many courageous hardships, in spite of our very different situations? Can these inspire us? What of those in troubled parts of the world?
6. Does "the anxiety for all the churches" make senior pastoral office seem problematic as well as honorific?
7. Do we ever mistakenly regard Paul as humorless? (cf. vv. 32–33).

6. Paul's visions and revelation, the climax of "the fool's speech" (12:1–13)

It is necessary to boast; nothing is to be gained by it, but I will go on to visions and revelations of the Lord. ² I know a person in Christ who fourteen years ago was caught up to the third heaven—whether in the body or out of the body I do not know; God knows. ³ And I know that such a person—whether in the body or out of the body I do not know; God knows— ⁴ was caught up into Paradise and heard things that are not to be told, that no mortal is permitted to repeat. ⁵ On behalf of such a one I will boast, but on my own behalf I will not boast, except of my weaknesses. ⁶ But if I wish to boast, I will not be a fool, for I will be speaking the truth. But I refrain from it, so that no one may think better of me than what is seen in me or heard from me, ⁷ even considering the exceptional character of the revelations. Therefore, to keep[a] me from being too elated, a thorn was given me in the flesh, a messenger of Satan to torment me, to keep me from being too elated. ⁸ Three times I appealed to the Lord about this, that it would leave me, ⁹ but he said to me, "My grace is sufficient for you, for power is made perfect in weakness." So, I will boast all the more gladly of my weaknesses, so that the power of Christ may dwell in me. ¹⁰ Therefore I am content with weaknesses, insults, hardships, persecutions, and calamities for the sake of Christ; for whenever I am weak, then I am strong.

¹¹ I have been a fool! You forced me to it. Indeed you should have been the ones commending me, for I am not at all inferior

> to these super-apostles, even though I am nothing. ¹² The signs of a true apostle were performed among you with utmost patience, signs and wonders and mighty works. ¹³ How have you been worse off than the other churches, except that I myself did not burden you? Forgive me this wrong!

In vv. 1-6, Paul describes how God had transported him to paradise, where he heard words "that are not to be told, that no mortal is permitted to repeat." The boasting of his opponents has "forced upon him" his response, even though it is "an unprofitable exercise" (vv. 1, 11).[91] Visions and revelations are both in the plural. They are private and are between Paul and God. Barnett suggests that the phrase is "perhaps dismissive in intent," while Guthrie calls his words a "parody" of language about visionary experiences.[92] In vv. 7-9, Paul boasts of his extreme weakness, his "thorn in the flesh," "a messenger of Satan to torment me."

The section of vv. 2-4 forms an integrated unit, pointing back fourteen years from 55 AD to AD 42, when Paul probably experienced his time in Cilicia or Syria shortly after his conversion and commission. He seems unwilling to identify himself with the man (Greek, *anthrōpos*) who had the visions, referring to him in the third person. The man was "caught up" (Greek, *harpazō*, in the aorist passive indicative, *was caught up*) to the "third heaven" (v. 2), which in v. 4 is called "paradise." Most commentators, including Thrall, insist that the man must be Paul himself. Thrall even considers four alternative suggestions, which she rightly dismisses.[93] She also rejects four suggestions about his use of the third person, concluding that Paul simply wants to avoid seeming arrogant.[94] His inclusion of "words never to be told" may be his explanation of why he has never referred to this incident before. The amount of speculation about these verses explains Guthrie's comment, "The passage before us stands as one of the most debated in Pauline literature."[95]

"Paradise" originally denoted parks or gardens belonging to the Persian king but was used in the LXX to denote the Garden of Eden (Gen 2:8; 13:10; Ezek 28:13; 31:8). In apocalyptic literature, it denoted transcendent places of blessedness (1 En. 32:3). It could denote the presence of God.

---

91. Barnett, *Second Corinthians*, 556.
92. Barnett, *Second Corinthians* 558; Guthrie, *2 Corinthians*, 580.
93. Thrall, *2 Corinthians*, 778-79.
94. Thrall, *2 Corinthians*, 781-82.
95. Guthrie, *2 Corinthians*, 576.

Paul disclaims knowledge of whether such a vision took place in or out of the body. He stresses that such a vision lies outside normal experience. The one thing that he can remember was that he heard "unutterable words" (Greek, *arrēta rhemata*), i.e., things that cannot be expressed. Paul could not express them and was not authorized to speak them.

In v. 6a, Paul is hypothetical ("if I wish to boast"), but v. 6b is emphatic, "I refrain from it." This boasting from which he refrains concerns the "man" who was caught up to paradise, i.e., himself. The opponents can "see" and "hear" Paul's weakness and his preaching of Christ.[96] These are integral with each other. Barnett continues, "Ironically, Paul turns their 'boast' back on them; they are in his ironic words, 'superlative' apostles, to whom, however, he is not 'inferior' (11:5; 12:11)."[97] They boast that they are "superior" in rhetorical power and much else. But in v. 7 Paul introduces his notorious phrase "To keep me from being too elated, a thorn (Greek, *skolops*) was given me in the flesh (Greek, *tē sarki*), a messenger of Satan to torment me." The "thorn" was given (Greek, *edothē*) to Paul so that he would not be consumed with self-importance. It was positive and transformative. Barnett comments, "Few questions in the N.T. have excited greater interest. From early times to the present scholars continue to give their answers."[98] Martin observes, "Discussion of this verse will not lead the exegete to certainty regarding the identity of Paul's 'thorn in the flesh.'"[99] Hughes writes, the thorn "is another one of those questions which on the evidence available must remain unanswered."[100]

Thrall (and Guthrie) categorize the suggestions into those that identify the "thorn" with a psychological condition (four types); those that identify it with opponents in Corinth (two); and those that identify it with physical illness or some disability (more than four suggestions).[101] One of the most specific is Harris, who understands "three times" (Greek, *tris*) to mean "three *different* times" or on three separate occasions, which would include Paul's affliction in Asia (2 Cor 1:8–11).[102] The vast majority of modern commentators, however, agree that "in the flesh" denotes a physical torment. Satan is

---

96. Barnett, *Second Corinthians*, 565.
97. Barnett, *Second Corinthians*, 565.
98. Barnett, *Second Corinthians*, 568.
99. Martin, *2 Corinthians*, 411.
100. Hughes, *Second Corinthians*, 442.
101. Thrall, *2 Corinthians*, 809–17.
102. Harris, *Second Corinthians*, 860–61.

often thought of as a bringer of illness, and Greek *skolops* (thorn) means a sharp splinter or stake. While the main VSS, including NJB and NIV retain "thorn in the flesh," the NEB translates "a sharp physical pain" (which it puts into quotation marks), and J. B. Phillips, "a physical handicap." Hughes suggests, "an unpleasant and humiliating physical ailment."[103] Among the physical disabilities, epilepsy and ophthalmia cannot be ruled out, although they remain speculative suggestions. Harris's suggestion of specific events in Paul's life perhaps remain among the most credible.

It is noteworthy that in v. 9 Paul pleaded (Greek, *parakaleō*) with God three times to remove this tormenting "thorn." But God did not give a positive answer, even to Paul. This should warn us against crude or simplistic views of prayer. God's reply was: "My grace is sufficient for you, for power is made perfect in weakness." This constitutes a key point. If God's power is really made perfect (Greek, *teleitai*) *in weakness* (Greek, *en astheneia*), no wonder that Paul boasts in his weakness! Barnett writes, "Here is the ultimate revelation, which stands for all time. Paul no longer prays for the removal of the 'thorn.' That lies in the past.... The grace of God is not only for the beginning of the Christian life; it is for the beginning, the middle, and the end."[104]

Barnett adds, "Through the pain of the 'thorn,' Paul was to learn that we get no lasting glory here, least of all through dramatic religious experiences, though they appear glorious and laden with power. There is a 'power' which brings elation; but it is the power of the flesh, not the power of Christ."[105] He continues, "This is not, we emphasise, merely a 'devotional thought.' It is at the very heart of the gospel and the argument of this letter."[106] Grace is apprehended only in the awareness of our weakness. The grace and power of God interlock with human lives at the point of mortal weakness. This is like Paul's earlier thought that the treasure of the gospel is conveyed as if through frail earthenware jars (4:7) "in order that it may be made clear that this extraordinary power comes from God and not from us."[107]

Paul's conclusion to "the Fool's Speech": "Therefore I am content with weaknesses, insults, hardships, persecutions, and calamities for the sake of Christ; for whenever I am weak then am I strong" (v. 10). Here he shows

---

103. Hughes, *Second Corinthians*, 448.
104. Barnett, *The Message of 2 Corinthians*, 178.
105. Barnett, *The Message of 2 Corinthians*, 178.
106. Barnett, *The Message of 2 Corinthians*, 179.
107. Guthrie, *2 Corinthians*, 593.

PART II: EXEGESIS

why such burdensome and unpleasant experiences give him such delight and cause for boasting, and do not destroy his contentment. In Homer, Odysseus may glory in his guile, and Achilles in his strength, but Paul glories in his weaknesses. Thus, he glories also in insults or indignities (Greek, *en hybresin*), in persecutions, in calamities or crises (Greek, *en anagkais*), persecutions (Greek, *diōgmois*, which Danker renders "a program or process designed to harass or oppress someone"), and stressful situations (Greek, *stenochōriais*).[108] So often, today, when regular ministry is interrupted by crises (illness, interruptions, or any unexpected situation) we are tempted to resent them. Paul gloried in them! We may compare this list with Rom 8:35, where Paul lists troubles that cannot separate us from God's love. All of these are accepted "for the sake of Christ" (Greek, *hyper Christou*). Greek *hyper* with the genitive case usually suggests the idea of advantage, i.e., for Christ's sake. The important reference to Christ prevents this list becoming a self-centered, self-help, list. It is as Christ's apostle that Paul glories in his weaknesses. Furnish observes, "Paul . . . is doing this *because of Christ*, as an apostolic agent of Christ's power."[109]

Verses 11–13 form an epilogue to Paul's "fool's speech." He states that he has donned the mantel of the "fool" only because his opponents forced him to it (v. 11). But again he insists that he lacks nothing that the false apostles try to claim for themselves. Barnett observes, "Paul ironically mirrors the superior/inferior vocabulary of these opponents: 'In nothing was I inferior to these "superlative" apostles.'"[110] In view of his reluctance to make claims about his visionary experience, it may seem strange that he includes among "the signs of the apostle" "signs, wonders, and miracles." These are authentic signs in Acts after Pentecost, and Harris notes that the three phenomena are regularly grouped together: signs offer validation; wonders elicit awe; and miracles display God's power.[111] Paul does not withdraw anything that he has said; these are less prominent than his humble apostolic service. Indeed, he speaks of his endurance or fortitude (Greek, *hypomonē*) and reasserts his own nothingness. He insists on his work as apostle not "burdening" them financially.

---

108. BDAG, 253; and Guthrie, *2 Corinthians*, 596.
109. Furnish, *II Corinthians*, 351 (his italics).
110. Barnett, *Second Corinthians*, 578.
111. Harris, *Second Corinthians*, 875.

Questions for reflection

1. Paul seems relatively unconcerned about his "visions." Do we sometimes place too high an evaluation on Christians (past or present) who lay claim to such experiences?
2. Do we, unlike Paul, regard "thorns," whether physical illness, interruptions to our regular work, or psychological problems, as annoying hindrances to God's work, or as possible God-sent opportunities to learn and grow? Can even the "humiliating" be good for us?
3. Do we always expect that God will give positive answers to our prayers, in spite of negative replies to Paul's repeated pleas?
4. In what are we most to glory? Is this really in our "weaknesses"?

7. Preparation for Paul's third visit to Corinth and final greetings (12:14—13:4)

[14] Here I am, ready to come to you this third time. And I will not be a burden, because I do not want what is yours but you; for children ought not to lay up for their parents, but parents for their children. [15] I will most gladly spend and be spent for you. If I love you more, am I to be loved less? [16] Let it be assumed that I did not burden you. Nevertheless (you say) since I was crafty, I took you in by deceit. [17] Did I take advantage of you through any of those whom I sent to you? [18] I urged Titus to go, and sent the brother with him. Titus did not take advantage of you, did he? Did we not conduct ourselves with the same spirit? Did we not take the same steps?

[19] Have you been thinking all along that we have been defending ourselves before you? We are speaking in Christ before God. Everything we do, beloved, is for the sake of building you up. [20] For I fear that when I come, I may find you not as I wish, and that you may find me not as you wish; I fear that there may perhaps be quarreling, jealousy, anger, selfishness, slander, gossip, conceit, and disorder. [21] I fear that when I come again, my God may humble me before you, and that I may have to mourn over many who previously sinned and have not repented of the impurity, sexual immorality, and licentiousness that they have practiced.

13 This is the third time I am coming to you. "Any charge must be sustained by the evidence of two or three witnesses." [2] I warned those who sinned previously and all the others, and I warn

them now while absent, as I did when present on my second visit, that if I come again, I will not be lenient— ³ since you desire proof that Christ is speaking in me. He is not weak in dealing with you, but is powerful in you. ⁴ For he was crucified in weakness, but lives by the power of God. For we are weak in him, but in dealing with you we will live with him by the power of God.

Paul's first visit to Corinth was in c.50 AD when he founded the church and stayed there eighteen months. He refers to a second, "painful," visit in 2 Cor 2:1–2, which would be in the Spring of 54. Writing in 54/55 he states his intention of paying a third visit to Corinth (12:14–15 and 19). He hopes that face-to-face encounter will enable him to set outstanding matters in order. Those who insist on making trouble will be called to account. After his first visit he calls his converts his spiritual children (1 Cor 4:14–15). We observed in our commentary that this had nothing to do with authoritarianism or control (as E. Castelli tried to maintain) but was an expression of familial care and affection. He affirms this in 2 Cor 6:13 and in chapter 12.

Paul is forced to talk again about money. He consistently refuses to charge and to accept a fee for his ministry. He is their spiritual father; not a patron. He must also rebut the accusation that he does receive money, but "through the back door, via his co-workers."[112] Paul's statement, "I will not be a burden" (v. 14) is bound up with his observations about parents and children. Children, he says, ought not to save up for their parents, but parents for their children (still v. 14). This was widely regarded as an axiom in the Greco-Roman world (e.g., in Seneca). Paul begins this sentence with Greek *idou*, look! Guthrie renders this "pay attention!" and the NRSV, "Here I am."[113] In v. 15, he expounds this in terms of a father's love. With deep personal emotion, he asks, "If I love you more, am I to be loved less?" He tells them that he thinks of them ceaselessly. He will "spend and be spent" for them (v. 15).

In vv. 16–18, he addresses the disgraceful suggestion that he goes craftily behind their backs to obtain money through his colleagues such as Titus. This accusation shows how low the "super-apostles" could stoop. Paul calmly responds to his own rhetorical question with Greek *estō*, let it be, which NRSV renders "let it be assumed" (v. 16a). The Greek words *panourgos* and *dolō* intensify each other to mean the use of manipulative, crafty, guile, and fraud or deceit. He asks rhetorically, "Did I take

---

112. Barnett, *Second Corinthians*, 583.
113. Guthrie, *2 Corinthians*, 609.

advantage of you [or cheat you] through any of those whom I sent to you?" (v. 17). Paul reiterates that he urged Titus to visit them (v. 18). Some (including Guthrie) understand "spirit" in this verse to refer to the Holy Spirit, but Furnish and most writers take it in the anthropological sense almost as "mind" as in 7:13.[114]

12:19 can be understood as a question (NRSV) or as a statement. The NRSV's "all along" probably rightly translates the Greek *ēdē*, which often means "for a long time." Perhaps they have been assuming that Paul's motive was a public defense of himself, i.e., virtually commending himself! But Paul's concern is accountability and integrity. He will speak "before God" (v. 19). As in 1 Corinthians, everything is for "your building up" (Greek, *hyper tēs hymōoikodomēs*).[115] Paul does what he does because the Corinthians are dear to him. However, in v. 29 he expresses the fear that "I may not find you as I wish" when the third visit occurs. They may disappoint one another (v. 20a); they might have dysfunctional relationships (v. 20b); and Paul might feel ashamed again, if he has to face blatant immorality in the church (v. 21).

In 1:23—2:1, he wanted to "spare" them, wishing not to cause emotional turmoil. He also had to write the "painful" letter. So his misgivings are understandable, although they had responded positively to Titus' visit. The Greek aorist subjunctive *heurō* expresses uncertainty, "I may find" (v. 20). "Quarreling, jealousy, anger, selfishness, slander, gossip, conceit, and disorder" are exactly the problems that Paul faced in 1 Corinthians, when he wrote, around AD 54.[116] If such a state still persisted, Paul will feel humbled. It would be as if much of his work has been in vain. He also fears further conflict in the church. What he longs for is that offenders will genuinely mourn and repent, especially over "sexual immorality and licentiousness" (v. 21). The passage reminds us of his concerns in 1 Cor 5:1-8.[117] His concern extends to 13:1-4. Hughes suggests that expulsion from the church might be possible.[118]

In 13:1-10, Paul envisages his next visit to be one of stern accountability. This is his third visit after his long eighteen-week stay and his brief "sorrowful" visit (2 Cor 2:1-2) in about 54 AD. On this third visit he will

---

114. Guthrie, *2 Corinthians*, 616; Furnish, *II Corinthians*, 560.
115. Mitchell, *Paul and the Rhetoric of Reconciliation*.
116. Thiselton, *1 Corinthians*, 1-28, and Thiselton, *First Epistle*, 1-41.
117. Thiselton, *First Epistle*, 384-408.
118. Hughes, *Second Epistle*, 472-73.

receive the collection for Jerusalem. He also appeals to Scripture for witnesses to validate his accusation. His biblical quotation comes from Deut 19:15 (LXX). The unique requirement in Israelite law is that at least two witnesses are needed for a conviction. "Two or three" (v. 1) means at least two. In Greek, the future passive of *histēmi* (*sustained*, NRSV) has the sense of "upheld" or "established" or even "validated."[119] But who are the witnesses? Commentators suggest God, Timothy, Titus, or members of the church. Harris and Guthrie understand the double witness of Paul's two warnings.[120] Hughes endorses the suggestion of Chrysostom and Calvin that Paul alludes to his two comings to Corinth.[121]

In 13:2–3, Paul underlines that his third visit goes beyond his previous warnings. This time persistent sinners will not be spared. Paul will not be lenient toward "those who have continued in their former sinning."[122] Paul's opponents demand proof that Christ is speaking through him. The cruciform Christ may seem "weak," but he also exemplifies the power of God (v. 4). Hughes comments, "Rebellion against an appointed minister is rebellion against the higher power that appointed him."[123] As in 1 Cor 1–4, the two poles of weakness and power come to view.

Questions for reflection

1. God's fatherly care does not suffer from unfortunate authoritarianism but stems from deep affection and love. Are we repelled by unfortunate examples of authoritarianism? Are we prepared to be cared for by our pastoral leaders?

2. Are we bothered by questions about "fees" for Christian work? Do we see such issues in the light of God's generous grace?

3. Are we sometimes too quick to accuse a fellow Christian of manipulative behavior? Might it help to understand the stresses and strains behind their behavior?

4. When Christians have been forgiven for wrongdoing, does accountability sometimes still remain for the consequences of their actions?

---

119. Danker, BDAG, 482.
120. Harris, *Second Corinthians*, 908; Guthrie, *2 Corinthians*, 631.
121. Hughes, *Second Corinthians*, 474.
122. Furnish, *II Corinthians*, 570.
123. Hughes, *Second Corinthians*, 477.

5. Do we respect the law that demands "at least two witnesses" in cases of accusation? Or do we listen too readily to gossip?

8. An authentication of faith, the purpose of Paul's letter, and final greetings and benediction (13:5-13)

> [5] Examine yourselves to see whether you are living in the faith. Test yourselves. Do you not realize that Jesus Christ is in you?—unless, indeed, you fail to meet the test! [6] I hope you will find out that we have not failed. [7] But we pray to God that you may not do anything wrong—not that we may appear to have met the test, but that you may do what is right, though we may seem to have failed. [8] For we cannot do anything against the truth, but only for the truth. [9] For we rejoice when we are weak and you are strong. This is what we pray for, that you may become perfect. [10] So I write these things while I am away from you, so that when I come, I may not have to be severe in using the authority that the Lord has given me for building up and not for tearing down.
>
> [11] Finally, brothers and sisters, farewell. Put things in order, listen to my appeal, agree with one another, live in peace; and the God of love and peace will be with you. [12] Greet one another with a holy kiss. All the saints greet you.
>
> [13] The grace of the Lord Jesus Christ, the love of God, and the communion of[e] the Holy Spirit be with all of you.

Guthrie writes, "Some in the Corinthian church have demanded proof of the authoritative source of Paul's ministry and message, and as we have seen, the apostle points to the manifestation of resurrection power in their midst as proof. Now Paul turns the tables on the Corinthians, suggesting that they need to examine themselves!"[124] In vv. 5-6 he says, "Examine yourselves to see whether you are living in the faith. Test yourselves." The reality of Christ's living in their lives ought to be self-evident, if they are really Christians. It remains Paul's hope that "we have not failed" (v. 6). If they are to be authentic, they must truly be "in Christ." Paul uses the opportunity to teach them something about Christ, who was crucified, lives and is powerful among them.[125] The Corinthians must not forget that Christ suffered and died. In v. 6, the words are "ironic rather than

---

124. Guthrie, *2 Corinthians*, 637.
125. Barnett, *Second Corinthians*, 604.

pessimistic."[126] Will the Corinthians prove themselves? If the answer is "yes," they will approve Paul.

Second, in v. 7, Paul states that he prays to God that they will do good, not evil. From vv. 7 and 8 Paul becomes more positive and optimistic. In v. 8, he says that he can do nothing against the truth, but only for the truth. Chrysostom understood "the truth" to mean "the facts of the situation in Corinth; most others take "truth" to mean "the truth of the gospel."[127] The next verse, "That you may become more perfect" (NRSV) really means (Greek, *katartizō*) "mended," "thoroughly put back together in order," or "put to rights," although the actual Greek word *katartisis* occurs only here in the New Testament.[128] Here it means, "restored to their proper Christian life."

In v. 10, Paul reiterates that his purpose in writing was to ensure the spiritual and moral restoration of the church in Corinth. He writes when he is absent, as if he were there! He has the authority of the Lord "for building up and not for tearing down." This is the context for Paul's being "severe."

Third, in vv. 11–13, Paul turns to his "farewell" (NRSV) or "good-bye" (NEB; NIV; KJV/AV; Phillips), although Greek *chairete* can also be translated "rejoice" or "we wish you joy" (NJB; Furnish). Again, he uses the Greek word *katartizesthe*, "put [things] in order" (NRSV), "mend," or "put to rights." He also uses the word "appeal" (Greek, *parakaleō*). Paul makes his appeal that all may "agree with one another and live in peace." This is exactly what he appealed for in 1 Cor 1:10. Several phrases are identical between the two passages, including Greek *to auto phroneite*, where he wants them to take the same side, or be of one mind, and not to side with those who supposedly lead party cliques in the name of Peter, Apollos, and Paul (either in reality or under hypothetical names to preserve anonymity, as Hall argues). He prays that the God of love and peace will be with them. He adds in v. 12, "Greet one another with a holy kiss." Thrall writes that in the ancient world "Kisses were exchanged at greeting and parting" and the Christian element was to exchange "a holy kiss."[129] For them it was also a sign of family commitment (or of brotherhood and sisterhood) and respect. It was the outward sign of the fellowship of (i.e., from) the Holy Spirit.

---

126. Barnett, *Second Corinthians*, 609.
127. Thrall, *2 Corinthians*, 896–97.
128. Thrall, *2 Corinthians*, 898–99; Guthrie, *2 Corinthians*, 644–45.
129. Thrall, *2 Corinthians*, 912.

Finally in the last verse Paul prays "the words of the grace," i.e., the Trinitarian benediction made so familiar by Christian liturgies. He prays that grace (Greek, *charis*) may flow from Christ; that love (Greek, *agapē*) may flow from God; and that the fellowship (Greek, *koinonia*) or their community solidarity and consciousness of it may flow from the Holy Spirit. Guthrie comments, "Paul ends the letter with a beautiful, balanced, tripartite blessing, which has been celebrated as the most robust expression of the interworking of the Trinity in the NT."[130] Lionel S. Thornton rightly insists that the Greek word for "fellowship" cannot mean mere "companionship," but denotes the close bonds that unite the Christian community, which the Holy Spirit alone gives and makes possible.[131]

Questions for reflection

1. As Christians, we are obligated to test where we stand. Do we merely test ourselves at Lent and perhaps New Year's Day? Is our self-testing regular, or may we fall into the opposite temptation of undue introspection and lack of trust in God?
2. Does anything in our local church or community need "mending" or "putting to rights"?
3. Do we encourage or discourage splinter-groups in our church from whatever motive?
4. Are there times in our worship when we use tangible ways of greeting fellow Christians with respect and affection?
5. When we pray "the grace" together, can it become a mere routine?
6. Do we tend to pray merely for intimacy with the Holy Spirit, or also that the Holy Spirit may produce and strengthen the solidarity that binds together the whole fellowship of our community?

---

130. Guthrie, *2 Corinthians*, 652.
131. Thornton, *The Common Life in the Body of Christ*, 66–965.

BIBLIOGRAPHY

Ashwin, Angela. *The Book of a Thousand Prayers*. Grand Rapids: Zondervan, 1996.
Austin, John L. *How to Do Things with Words*. Oxford: Oxford University Press, 1962.
Barnett, Paul. *The Message of 2 Corinthians*. Leicester, UK: IVP, 1988.
———. *The Second Epistle to the Corinthians*. New International Commentary. Grand Rapids: Eerdmans, 1997.
Barrett, C. K. *The Second Epistle to the Corinthians*. London: Black, 1973.
Barth, Karl. *The Resurrection of the Dead*. ET. London: Hodder, 1933.
Beale, G. K. "The Old Testament Background of Reconciliation in 2 Corinthians 5–7 and Its Bearing on the Literary Problem of 2 Corinthians 6:14–7:1." *New Testament Studies* 35 (1989) 550–81.
Beasley-Murray, George. "Introduction." In *The Second Epistle to the Corinthians*. *The Interpreter's Bible*, vol. 10. Nashville: Abingdon, 1953.
Best, Ernest. "Apostolic Authority?" *Journal for the Study of the New Testament* 27 (1986) 2–25.
Betz, Hans Dieter, and G. W. MacRae. *2 Corinthians 8 and 9: A Commentary on Two Administrative Letter of the Apostle Paul*. Philadelphia: Fortress, 1985.
Bjerkelund, C. J. *Parakalō: Form, Funktion und Sinn der Parakalō-Sätze in der paulinischen Briefen*. Oslo: Universitetsforlaget, 1967.
Bray, Gerald, ed. *1–2 Corinthians*. Ancient Christian Commentary on Scripture. Downers Grove, IL: IVP, 1999.
Brightman, Edgar. *A Philosophy of Religion*. London: Skeffington, n.d.
Brown, Francis, S. R. Driver, and Charles A. Briggs. *Hebrew and English Lexicon*. Lafayette, IN: Associated Publishers, 1980.
Bruce, F. F. *The Pauline Circle*. Exeter, UK: Paternoster, 1985.
Brümmer, Vincent. *A Personal God*. Cambridge: Cambridge University Press, 1992.
———. *What Are We Doing When We Pray?* Farnham, UK: Ashgate, 2008.
Bultmann, Rudolf. *Theology of the New Testament*, vol.1. ET. London: SCM, 1952.
Castelli, E. A. *Imitating Paul: A Discussion of Power*. Louisville: Westminster/John Knox, 1991.
Cerfaux, L. *The Church in the Theology of St Paul*. Freiburg: Herder, 1959.

BIBLIOGRAPHY

Chrysostom, John. "Homilies in the Second Epistle to the Corinthians." In *Nicene and Post-Nicene Fathers, First Series*, vol. 12. Translated by Talbot Chambers; edited by Philip Schaff. Buffalo, NY: CLC, 1889.

Clarke, Andrew D. *Secular and Christian Leadership in Corinth: A Socio-Historical & Exegetical Study of 1 Corinthians 1-6*. Leiden: Brill, 1993.

Collins, J. N. *Diakonia: Reinterpreting the Ancient Sources*. New York: Oxford University Press, 1990.

Collins, R. F. "Reflections on One Corinthians as a Hellenistic letter." In *The Corinthian Correspondence*, edited by R. Bieringer, 39-61. Leuven: Leuven University Press, 1996.

Crafton, Jeffrey A. *The Agency of the Apostle: A Dramatistic Analysis of Paul's Responses to Conflict in 2 Corinthians*. JSNTSup 51. Sheffield, UK: Sheffield Academic Press, 1991.

Cullmann, Oscar. *Christ and Time: The Primitive Christian Conception of Time and History*. London: SCM, 1951.

———. *The Earliest Christian Confessions*. ET. London: Lutterworth, 1949.

Danker, F. W. "Paul's Debt to the *De Corona* of Demosthenes: A Study of Rhetorical Techniques in Second Corinthians." In *Persuasive Artistry*, edited by D. F. Watson, 262-80. Sheffield, UK: JSOT Press, 1991.

———. *A Greek-English Lexicon of the New Testament and Other Early Christian Literature*. BADG, 3rd ed. Chicago: University of Chicago Press, 2000.

Davies, W. D. *Paul and Rabbinic Judaism*. London: SPCK, 1958.

Deissmann, Adolf. *Light from the Ancient East*. ET. London: Hodder, 1911.

Denney, James. *The Death of Christ: Its Place and Interpretation in the New Testament*. London: Hodder, 1922.

———. *The Second Epistle to the Corinthians*. London: Hodder & Stoughton, 1894.

Dodd, C. H. "The Mind of Paul." In *New Testament Studies*, 67-128. Manchester: Manchester University Press, 1953.

Dumbrell, W. J. "The Newness of the New Covenant: The Logic of the Argument in 2 Corinthians 3." *Reformed Theological Review* 63 (2002) 61-84.

Dunn, James D. G. *The Theology of Paul the Apostle*. Edinburgh: T. & T. Clark, 1998.

Eckstein, H-J. *Der Begriff Syneidēsis bei Paulus*. Tübingen: Mohr, 1983.

Ellis, E. Earle. "II Corinthians V:1-10 in Pauline Eschatology." *New Testament Studies* 6 (1960) 211-24.

———. "Paul and His Co-Workers." In *Prophecy and Hermeneutic in Early Christianity*, 3-22. Grand Rapids: Eerdmans, 1978.

Engels, Donald. *Roman Corinth: An Alternative Model for the Classical City*. Chicago: University of Chicago Press, 1990.

Evans, Donald D. *The Logic of Self-Involvement*. London: SCM, 1963.

Fitzgerald, J. T. *Cracks in an Earthen Vessel: An Examination of Catalogues of Hardships in the Corinthian Correspondence*. SBLDS, 99. Atalanta: Scholars, 1988.

Furnish, Victor P. *II Corinthians*. Anchor Bible. New York: Doubleday, 1984.

———. "Corinthians, Second Letter to the." In *Dictionary of Biblical Interpretation*, edited by John H. Hayes, 223-27. Nashville: Abingdon, 1999.

Gale, Herbert M. *The Use of Analogy in the Letters of Paul*. Philadelphia: Westminster, 1964.

Garland, D. E. *2 Corinthians*. Nashville: Broadman, 1999.

Georgi, Dieter. *Die Geschichte der Kollekte des Paulus für Jerusalem*. Hamburg: Theologische Forschung, 1965.

BIBLIOGRAPHY

———. *Remembering the Poor: The History of Paul's Collection for Jerusalem*. ET. Nashville: Abingdon, 1992.
Gooch, Peter D. "Conscience in 1 Corinthians 8 and 10." *New Testament Studies* 33 (1987) 244–54.
Gunkel, Hermann. *The Influence of the Holy Spirit*. Minneapolis: Fortress, 2008.
Guthrie, George H. *2 Corinthians*. Grand Rapids: Baker Academic, 2015.
Guthrie, W. K. C. *The Sophists*. Cambridge: Cambridge University Press, 1971.
Hafemann, Scott J. *2 Corinthians*. Grand Rapids: Zondervan, 2000.
———. "'Self-Commendation' and Apostolic Legitimacy in 2 Corinthians: A Pauline Dialectic?" *New Testament Studies* 36 (1990) 66–88.
———. *Suffering and the Spirit: An Exegetical Study of II Corinthians 2:14–33*. 1986. Reprint, Eugene, OR: Wipf and Stock, 2011.
Hendry, George. *The Holy Spirit in Christian Theology*. London: SCM, 1966.
Hodgson, R. "Paul the Apostle and First-Century Tribulation Lists." *Zeitschrift für die neutestamentliche Wissenschaft und die Kunde der älteren Kirche* 74 (1983) 59–80.
Hall, David R. *The Unity of the Corinthian Correspondence*. JSNTSup 251. London: T. & T. Clark, 2003.
Hamilton, Neil Q. *The Holy Spirit and Eschatology in Paul*. SJT Occasional Papers. Edinburgh: Oliver & Boyd, 1957.
Hanson, Anthony T. *Studies in Paul's Technique and Theology*. London: SPCK, 1974.
Harrington, D. J. "Paul and Collaborative Ministry." *New Theological Review* 3 (1990) 62–71.
Harris, Murray. "2 Corinthians 5:1–10: A Watershed in Paul's Eschatology." *Tyndale Bulletin* 22 (1971) 32–57.
———. *The Second Epistle to the Corinthians*. NIGTC. Grand Rapids: Eerdmans, 2005.
Hodge, Charles. *The Second Epistle to the Corinthians*. London: Banner of Truth, 1959.
Hogg, A. G. *Redemption from This World*. Edinburgh: T. & T. Clark, 1924.
Holl, Karl. "Der Kirchenbegriff des Paulus in seinem Verhältnis zu dem der Urgemeinde." In *Gesammelte Aufsä6tze zur Kirchengeschichte, II: Der Osten*, edited by K. Holl, 44–67. Tübingen: Mohr, 1928.
Hughes, Philip E. *Paul's Second Epistle to the Corinthians*. London: Marshall, 1961.
Isaacs, Wilfrid H. *The Second Epistle of Paul to the Corinthians: A Study in Translations and an Interpretation*. Oxford: Oxford University Press, 1921.
Jewett, Robert. *Paul's Anthropological Terms: A Study of Their Use in Conflict Settings*. Leiden: Brill, 1971.
———. *Romans: A Commentary*. Minneapolis: Fortress, 2007.
Judge, Edwin A. "Paul's Boasting in Relation to Contemporary Professional Practice." *Australian Biblical Review* 16 (1968) 37–48.
Keener, C. S. *1–2 Corinthians*. New Cambridge Bible. Cambridge: Cambridge University Press, 2005.
Kent, J. H. *Corinth. Results of Excavatiions . . . Vol. VIII, Part III, The Inscriptions, 1926–1950*. Princeton: American School of Classical Studies, 1966.
Kleinknecht, K. T. *Der leidende Gerechtfertigte: Die altttestamentlich-jüdische Tradition vom 'leidenden Gerechten' und ihre Rezeption bei Paulus*. WUNT 11. Tübingen: Mohr, 1984.
Knox, W. L. *Paul and the Church of the Gentiles*. Cambridge: Cambridge University Press, 1939.
Kruse, Colin. *The Second Epistle of Paul to the Corinthians*. Leicester, UK: IVP, 1987.

BIBLIOGRAPHY

Kümmel, Werner G. *Introduction to the New Testament*. ET. London: SCM, 1966.
Lampe, G. W. H. *The Seal of the Spirit*. London: Longmans, 1951.
Lightfoot, J. B. *Notes on the Epistles* of St Paul. London: MacMillan, 1895.
Long, Frederick. "'The God of This Age' (2 Cor. 4:4) and Paul's Empire-Resisting Gospel at Corinth." In *The First Urban Churches*, Vol. 1, edited by James R. Harrison and L. Welborn, 219–69. Atlanta: Scholars, 2016.
Lossky, Vladimir. *The Mystical Theology of the Eastern Church*. Cambridge: James Clarke, 1991.
Lowe, J. "An Attempt to Detect Developments in St. Paul's Eschatology." *Journal of Theological Studies* 42 (1941) 129–42.
Malherbe, A. J. "The Beasts at Ephesus." *Journal of Biblical Literature* 87 (1968) 71–80.
Martin, Ralph P. *2 Corinthians*. WBC. Dallas: Word, 1991.
Metzger, Bruce. *A Textual Commentary on the Greek New Testament*. 4th ed. Stuttgart: United Bible Societies, 1992.
Meyer, H. A. W. *Critical and Exegetical Handbook to the Epistles to the Corinthians*. ET. New York: Funk & Wagnalls, 1890.
Mitchell, Margaret M. *Paul and the Rhetoric of Reconciliation*. Louisville: Westminster/John Knox, 1991.
Moltmann, Jürgen. *The Coming of God*. London: SCM, 1996.
Morris, Leon. *The Cross in the New Testament*. Grand Rapids: Eerdmans, 1965.
Murphy O'Connor, Jerome. *St Paul's Corinth: Texts and Archaeology*. Wilmington, DE: Glazier, 1995.
———. *The Theology of the Second Letter to the Corinthians*. Cambridge: Cambridge University Press, 1991.
Neufeld, Vernon H. *The Earliest Christian Confessions*. Leiden: Brill, 1963.
Ollrog, W. H. *Paulus und seine Mitarbeiter*. Neukirchen: Neukirchener, 1979.
Phillips, J. B. *Letters to Young Churches*. London: Bles, 1947.
Pierce, C. A. *Conscience in the New Testament*. London: SCM, 1955.
Plank, Karl A. *Paul and the Irony of Affliction*. Atalanta: Scholars, 1987.
Plummer, Alfred. *A Critical and Exegetical Commentary on the Second Epistle of St Paul to the Corinthians*. ICC. Edinburgh: T. & T. Clark, 1915.
Pogoloff, Stephen M. *Logos and Sophia: The Rhetorical Situation of 1 Corinthians*. Atlanta: Scholars, 1992.
Robertson, A. T. *Word Pictures in the New Testament*, Vol. 4. New York: Smith, 1931.
Robinson, John A. T. *The Body: A Study in Pauline Theology*. London: SCM, 1952.
Ryle, Gilbert. *Dilemmas*. Cambridge: Cambridge University Press, 1966.
Rupp, E. G., and B. Drewery. *Martin Luther*. London: Arnold, 1970.
Sampley, J. P. "Paul, His Opponents in 2 Corinthians 10–13, and the Rhetorical Handbooks." In *The Social World of Primitive Christianity and Judaism*, edited by J. Neusner et al., 37–48. Philadelphia: Fortress, 1988.
Savage, Timothy B. *Power through Weakness: Paul's Understanding of the Christian Ministry in 2 Corinthians*. SNTSMS 86. Cambridge: Cambridge University Press, 1996.
Schrage, W. "Leid, Kreuz und Eschaton. Die Peristasenkatalogge als Merkmale paulinischer theologia crucis and Eschatologie." *Evangelische Theologie* 34 (1974) 353–75.
Schweitzer, Albert. *The Mysticism of Paul the Apostle*. ET. London: Black, 1931.
Searle, John. *Expression and Meaning: Studies in the Theory of Speech Acts*. Cambridge: Cambridge University Press, 1979.
Spicq, C. *Theological Lexicon of the New Testament*. ET. Peabody, MA: Hendrickson, 1994.

Stowers, Stanley K. "*Peri Men Gar* and the Integrity of 2 Corinthians 8 and 9." *Novum Testamentum* 32 (1990) 340–48.
Strawson, P. F. *An Introduction to Logical Theory*. London: Methuen, 1963.
Swete, Henry B. *The Holy Spirit in the New Testament*. London: Macmillan, 1921.
Tasker, R. V. G. *The Second Epistle of Paul to the Corinthians*. London: Tyndale, 1958.
Taylor, Vincent. *The Person of Christ in New Testament Teaching*. London: Macmillan, 1958.
Theissen, Gerd. *The Social Setting of Pauline Christianity: Essays on Corinth*. 1982. Reprint, Eugene, OR: Wipf & Stock, 2004.
Thiselton, Anthony C. *1 Corinthians: A Shorter Exegetical & Pastoral Commentary*. Grand Rapids: Eerdmans, 2005.
———. *Doubt, Faith and Certainty*. Grand Rapids: Eerdmans, 2017.
———. *The First Epistle to the Corinthians*. NIGTC. Grand Rapids: Eerdmans, 2000.
———. *The Holy Spirit: In Biblical Teaching, through the Centuries and Today*. London: SPCK, 2013.
———. *Systematic Theology*. Grand Rapids: Eerdmans, 2015.
———. *Thiselton on Hermeneutics*. Grand Rapids: Eerdmans, 2006.
Thornton, Lionel S. *The Common Life in the Body of Christ*. London: Dacre, 1948.
Thrall, Margaret E. "The Pauline Use of *suneidēsis*." *New Testament Studies* 31 (1985) 161–88.
———. *The Second Epistle to the Corinthians*. 2 vols. ICC. Edinburgh: T. & T. Clark, 1994, 2004.
Travis, Stephen. *Christ and the Judgement of God*. 2nd ed. Milton Keynes, UK: Paternoster, 2008.
———. "Paul's Boasting in 2 Corinthians." *Studia Evangelica* 6 (1973) 527–32.
Watson, Francis. *Paul and the Hermeneutics of Faith*. London: T. & T. Clark, 2004.
Weiss, Johannes. *History of Primitive Christianity*. New York: Harper, 1937.
Welborn, L. L. *Paul, the Fool of Christ: A Study of 1 Corinthians 1–4 in the Comic-Philosophical Tradition*. London: T. & T. Clark, 2005.
Windisch, Hans. *Der zweite Korintherbrief*. Göttingen: Vandenhoeck & Ruprecht, 1924.
Witherington, Ben. *Conflict and Community in Corinth: A Socio-Rhetorical Commentary on 1 and 2 Corinthians*. Grand Rapids: Eerdmans, 1995.
Yinger, Kent L. *Paul, Judaism, and Judgement according to Deeds*. SNTSMS 105. Cambridge: Cambridge University Press, 1999.
Young, Frances M., and David F. Ford. *Meaning and Truth in 2 Corinthians*. 1987. Reprint, Eugene, OR: Wipf & Stock, 2008.

INDEX OF NAMES

Allo, E.-B., 38
Augustine, 45

Barnett, Paul, 3, 9, 11, 112–23, 127, 129–32
Barrett, C. K., 8–11, 23, 29, 31, 35, 36, 44, 45, 48, 52, 53, 59, 64, 65, 75, 83, 86, 89, 100, 101, 109, 110, 125
Barth, Karl, 117
Beale, G. K., 82
Beasley-Murray, George, 8
Betz, Hans Dieter, 11, 94, 96, 100, 101, 105–6
Bjerkelund, C. J., 100
Brightman, Edgar, 26
Bruce, F. F., 60
Bultmann, Rudolf, 22, 35, 38, 39, 53, 54, 63, 94, 101, 113

Calvin, John, 136
Castelli, Elizabeth, 97, 134
Chrysostom, John, 37, 40, 90, 97, 112, 136, 138
Cicero, 10
Clarke, Andrew, 43
Claudius, 7, 25
Clement of Rome, 107
Clement of Alexandria, 29
Collange, J. F., 39
Collins, J. N., 45, 96
Collins, R. F., 11

Crafton, Jeffrey, 19, 41
Cullmann, Oscar, 62, 63, 77, 106

Danker, Frederick, 45, 48, 52, 75, 78, 90, 132
Davies, W. D., 73
Deissmann, Adolf, 44, 75
Demosthenes, 10
Denney, James, 39, 75, 77, 86
Dodd, Charles H., 65
Dunn, James D. G., 59

Ellis, E. Earle, 65
Engels, Donald, 3, 42, 43, 96

Fitzgerald, J. T., 57, 78, 79
Ford, David F., 9, 11, 105, 109
Furnish, Victor, 28, 37, 41, 52, 53, 58, 59, 60, 75, 80, 94, 107, 109, 113, 126, 132, 135

Gale, Herbert M., 112
Geach, Peter, 84
Georgi, Dieter, 37, 98
Gregory of Nazianzus, 76
Gunkel, Hermann, 67
Guthrie, George, 9, 11, 34, 36, 38–40, 46–48, 55, 57, 58, 60, 66, 67, 74, 76, 79, 82, 85, 94, 95, 98, 102, 106, 114, 126, 137

INDEX OF NAMES

Hafemann, S. J., 44, 46, 57, 65, 78, 82
Hall, David R., 8–13, 34, 82, 94, 109, 119
Hamilton, Neill Q., 67
Harris, Murray, 25, 26, 44, 53, 60, 64, 89, 109, 132, 136
Hausrath, Adolf, 39
Hendry, George, 49
Héring, Jean, 9
Hodgson, R., 57
Hogg, A., G., 63, 69
Holl, Karl, 98
Hughes, Philip E., 10, 23, 39, 44, 53, 78, 102, 112, 113, 135

Isaacs, Wilfried, 25, 45, 64

Judge, E. A., 110, 125

Kleinknecht, K. T., 57
Knox, W. L., 65
Kümmel, Werner G., 108
Käsemann, Ernst, 12, 44

Lampe, Geoffrey, 32
Long, Frederick, 53
Lossky, Vladimir, 53
Luther, Martin, 45, 68

Manson, T. W., 9
Martin, Dale, 10, 40
Martin, Ralph, 23, 25, 64, 75, 85, 94, 98, 107, 111, 122, 130
Meeks, Wayne, 43
Metzger, Bruce M., 89, 116
Meyer, H. A. W., 39
Moltmann, Jürgen, 51
Moores, John D., 52
Morris, Leon, 75
Moule, C. F. D., 66
Munck, Johannes, 108
Murphy-O'Connor, Jerome, 10, 11

Neufeld, Vernon H., 106

Origen, 45

Peirce, C. A., 29
Phillips, J. B., 44, 111, 115
Philo, 22, 48
Plank, A., 57, 78
Plummer, Alfred, 20, 26, 28, 31, 34, 59, 60, 62, 64, 66, 78, 83, 85, 90, 104, 110
Plutarch, 40, 57
Pogoloff, Stephen, 43, 52, 96
Robertson, A. T., 39, 48, 52, 71, 75
Robinson, J. A. T., 112
Ryle, G., 65

Sampley, J. P., 110
Savage, Tim, 54, 55
Schrage, W., 57
Schweitzer, Albert, 59
Semler, J. S., 9, 39
Sevenster, J. N., 64
Spicq, C., 83
Spurgeon, Charles H., 88
Strabo, 37
Taylor, Vincent, 49
Theissen, Gerd, 10, 43, 97
Thiselton, Anthony C., 97
Thornton, Lionel S., 139
Thrall, Margaret, 9, 29, 39, 48, 50, 52, 53, 55, 56, 58, 59, 60, 64, 66, 71, 73, 75, 79, 82, 88, 89, 94–96, 100, 104, 113, 116
Travis, Stephen, 68, 125

United Bible Society Committee, the, 102, 116

Van der Brink, Gjisbert, 84

Weiss, Johannes, 73
Welborn, L. L., 118
Whiteley, Dennis, 75
Windisch, Hans, 9, 38, 125
Witherington, Ben, 11, 43, 94, 109, 110

Young, Frances M., 9, 11, 105, 109

Winter, Bruce, 53

INDEX OF SUBJECTS

abundance of God, 105
accountability to God, 68
accountability, 134
accusation, 79, 100
adulterating God's word, 41
affliction as light, 63
affliction in Asia, 26–27
agreement or harmony, 83
alliteration, 105
ambassador's message, 70
ambassadors for Christ, 73, 75, 77
Amen, 31, 33
another Jesus and another Spirit, 119
answered prayer, 41
Apostleship, 19–20, 44
Apostolic authority, 8, 80
apostolic credentials, 77, 78
apostolic eyewitnesses, 64
appeal, 100
Aquila and Priscilla, 7
Aramaic, 125
Asia, 37
audience-pleasing rhetoric, 52
authentic apostles, 43, 79, 80
authentication of faith, 137

Babbius Philinus, 43, 123
baptismal dying, 58
beloved covenant people, 85
betrothal language, 120
birch rods, 126

blindness, 12, 55
boasting in the Lord, 117
boasting in trials and weaknesses, 124, 127, 131
boasting or glorying, 29–30, 92, 118
boost beyond limits, 115
bricks, pottery, roof tiles, etc., 7
broken relationship, 74
building, 64
busy, bustling, business centre, 4

catalogue of afflictions, 57, 78, 82
caught up, 129
change of plan, 31
cheerful giver, 104
children as affectionate intimacy, 82
Christ as humiliated and crucified, 53
Christ's love, 71
Christ's victory, 40
Christ-union, eschatological status of, 72
clay jars, 57
clothing-on-over, 66
cold temperatures, 127
collection, the, 11, 15, 94–95, 97, 101, 103, 106
collegiality, 100
comfort, 23
coming to the end of our tether, 23
comparisons between human leaders, 115, 116
competence or sufficiency, 45

INDEX OF SUBJECTS

competition in athletics and music, 4, 5
competitiveness and consumerism, 42–43
compulsion, 71
confession, 105
confidence, faith, and belief, 59, 86
confrontation, 34
conscience, 29–30
contemptible speech, 114
corporate personality, 73
covenant or testament, 46
covenant promises, 85, 125
covering of the head or face, 48
co-workers with God, 76
cruciform Christ, the, 136
curse of the law, 76

Damascus, 127
dangers, 127
day of salvation, 77
death, putting to death, 58
death-threatening illness, 25
decision and courage, 111
defilement, 85
different Jesus and different gospel, 119
distress in Asia, 25
doctrinal themes, 13, 14
dying and rising with Christ, 59
dysfunctional relationships, 135

eagerness to clear themselves, 90
earthenware or terra-cotta jars, 57
Eden analogy, 120
election, 100
emotional turmoil, 34
encouraging report, 87
end or goal, 48
entrenched power of unbelief, 112
entrepreneurial skills and hopes, 5
Ephesus, 25
Erastus, 43, 123
eternal glory, 63
Exclusive Brethren, 82
faith, understandings of, 34, 67–68
false apostles, 9, 19–20, 52, 78, 80, 86, 112, 116, 121
favourable moment, 76–77

fear and trembling, 110
fellowship as communal, 139
finished, 75
first instalment or pledge, 67
first over the wall, 125
flight from Damascus, 125, 127
forgiveness, 36
fourteen years, 129
fragrance or fume, 40
frank speech, 81
future eternal glory, 62

generosity, 15, 104
gentle methods, 111
genuineness of apostolic ministry, 96
gift of Christ, 107
gladiators struggling in the arena, 118
glory in weakness, 132
glory of God in the face of Jesus, 49
glory to God, 105
glory, 63
glorying in human people, 117
gnosis and wisdom, 3
God as Almighty/omnipotent, 84
God as Father, 82
God as Judge, 68, 69
God who raises the dead, 67
God's righteousness, 76
godly jealousy, 121
gold, silver, or everyday material, 57
grace of God, the, 60, 95, 131
Greco-Roman world, 10, 22, 98, 122, 123
greeting, 20

hardening, 49
hardships, 61
Hebrew, Jewish, and Christian thought, 62
Hebrews, 125
Hellenistic dualism, 63
Holy Spirit, 21, 32, 45, 49, 52, 79, 139
human criteria, human point of view, 72
humility, 55

image of God, 53
Imperial cult, 53

INDEX OF SUBJECTS

imprisonments, beatings, hard labour, 126
in Christ, 59
inadequate adequacy, 41
income from tourism, business, etc., 4, 5
incompatible relationships, 82
intermediate state, 65
ironic reversal of boasting, 119–20, 130
irony, Paul's use of, 115, 122, 125, 130
Isthmian Games, 4, 5

jealousy, godly, 119–20
Jerusalem apostles, 125
Jerusalem church, the, 98, 106
Jesus Christ, 96
joy, courage, and hope, 92
justification by grace, 59
justification by sovereign grace, 3

kairos as favourable moment, 76–77
knowledge (*gnosis*), 79
knowledge, 121
knowledge, two kinds of, 73

labouring manually, 122, 127
last judgement, awaited with joy, 68
leadership in Corinth, 43
letters of commendation, 43–44
letters of stone, 47, 48
literary plural, 74
lone Christians, 21
Lord, 22, 24

Macedonia, 38, 87, 95
Macedonian churches, 95, 101, 107
manna, 98
manipulative, crafty, guile, 134
manuscripts of the early church, 11
meekness and gentleness of Christ, 110
mercies, 22
military metaphors, 14, 112
ministry (Greek, *diakonia*), 105
ministry as open, 71
ministry, Paul's concept of, 42, 45, 48, 52, 116
mismatching with unbelievers, 82
missionary pastor, 126

mixed marriages, 82
mocking and ridicule, 78
money, 86, 134
Moses and the veil, 47–48
motive, 100
mourning and sorrow, 88

nakedness, 64
new covenant, 14
new creation, 70
new troubles, 3
nonentities, 79
non-Pauline vocabulary, 11

offensive and defensive weapons, 79
open door, 37
openness, 48, 81
outward appearance, 71, 113

painful visit, 33, 134
parading in public, 40
paradise, 129
parody, 110, 119
parousia, time of, 66
participant or observer viewpoint, 65
participation in Christ, 59
partition theories, unlikely, 9, 10, 109
pastors and clergy, 80
patience and kindness, 78, 80
patrons and clients, 8, 122
Paul's apostolic authority, 109–10
perseverance, 60, 63
persistent sinners, 136
personal defence, 110
philosophers and rhetoricians, 123
physical disabilities, e.g. epilepsy, 131
pillar-apostles in Jerusalem, 79
poor but making rich, 80
poor, the, 95, 96, 105
pottery vessels, ministers as, 40
prayer and "the best", 26
prayer to God, 105
prayer, 106
preaching Christ, 52
preaching of the gospel, 60
preaching the gospel free of charge, 122
pressure, stress, affliction, 23

INDEX OF SUBJECTS

Priscilla and Aquila, 122
prohibition of mixtures, 82
promises, 13, 14, 31, 85
punishment, 35
purity and faithfulness, 120
putting things to right, 69

quarrelling, jealousy, selfishness, 135

reconciliation, 73, 74
repentance, 88
reputation, 78
rescue, 26
restoration, 84
restorative justice, 68, 69
resurrection body, the, 64
resurrection power, 137
resurrection with Christ, 24, 27, 67
reversal of sinners' situation, 74
rhetoric, 79, 118, 121
rival missionaries, 54
Roman colony, 5, 95
Roman Corinth as prosperous community, 4

Satan, 36, 78, 83, 129, 130
security and freedom, 22
seen and unseen, 63
self as visible only to God, 63
self-advertisement, 44
self-commendation, 78, 115
self-defence, 90
self-made-person-escapes humble origins, 43
self-promotion, 42, 46
self-promotion, 7
self-satisfaction or complacency, 7
separation, 83
severe letter, 33, 90
signs, wonders, and miracles, 130
Silas, 31
sin and the community, 35
sin-offering, 75
sleepless nights, 108-9, 126
social networks of influence, 8
soldiers' experience, 58
soul, so-called, 66

speech-act theory, 69
substitution and participation, 72
substitutionary sacrifice for sin, 75-76
success in its crude form, 43
sufferings of Christ, 23, 119
sufferings of the apostles, 57
synagogue, 126

Taurus Mountains, 127
tearful letter, the, 13
temple of the living God, 83
temporal contrast: present and future, 62
tent as temporary, 66
thanksgiving to God, 107
thanksgiving, 21
theology of resurrection, 60
third heaven, 129
third visit to Corinth, 134
thirty-nine lashes, 126
thorn in the flesh, 129-31
three times as three separate occasions, 130
Timothy, 31
Titus, 37, 99, 134
Titus as Gentile convert, 88
Titus, his joy at his report, 87, 91-92
transcendent power, 55
transformation, 49
transparent windows, 21
travel narrative, 87
travelling preachers, 12
treasure of the gospel, 57, 70
triumphal procession, 39, 40
triumphalism, false, 118, 119
Troas, 37
troubling visit, 88
truthful and honest, 79
two gospels and two lifestyles, 119
two or three, 136

union with Christ, 59
unity of the epistle, 9, 10
unrevised verdict, 69

vacillation or faithlessness, 33
veil as a symbol of brightness, 48
visible manifestation of God, 53

INDEX OF SUBJECTS

visions and revelations, 129
vocabulary, non-Pauline, 11

warm affection, 81
weakness and vulnerability, 57, 129, 131
wealthy Corinth, 7
weapons of warfare, 111

whips or ropes, 78
withdrawal from fellowship, 36
words never to be told, 129
workshop, 5
worldly, godless, and limiting, 111

zeal, 90

INDEX OF BIBLICAL REFERENCES

Genesis

1:3	54

Exodus

20:5	120
34:29–35	71

Leviticus

6:28	57
11:33	57
14:50	57
19:19	83
20:2	126
24:14	126
26:11–12	83

Deuteronomy

17:5–7	126
22:9	83

2 Samuel

7:8,	14, 83, 85

Psalms

67:4	68
96:10–13	68
98:2	4, 9, 68
111:9	105
115:1	60

Proverbs

3:4	100
9:7	78

Isaiah

45:21–22	69
49:8	76
50:10	55
52:11	83, 84
53:6,	9, 76
54:5–6	120
60:1–3	55
62:5	120

Jeremiah

3:14	120

Ezekiel

20:34	83

Hosea

2:19–20	120

Matthew

7:63	79
17:27	71

Mark

10:45	71
13:32	66

John

11:50	71

Acts

14:19–20	126
16:23	126
17:58	95

Romans

3–6	58
5:10–11	74
6:3–4	72
6:3–8	59
7:29	112
8:8	111
8:17	23, 84
8:22–23	67
8:23	32
8:32	32
8:35	132
12:17	71

1 Corinthians

1:12	113, 115
1:17	18, 119
1:22	23, 53
2:2	53
2:3–5	110
3:16–17	84
3:21–22	80
4:8–13	57, 78, 118–19
4:11–12	122
4:15	120
6:19	22, 84
7:11	74
7:12–15	83
8–10	83
8:1	79
8:11	53
9:1–18	80
9:3–14	122
10:21	83
11:15	71
12:3	54
12:13	59
14:18	71
15:3–8	64
15:31–32	25, 78
15:32–57	64
15:44–45	64
15:52	60
15:54	67
16:9	25

2 Corinthians

Throughout, also especially

1:9	55, 60
1:4, 8	34
4:4–6	54
4:10–11	23
5:1–4	64
5:18	74
11:7–11	80

Galatians

1:6	119
1:12, 16	79
1:16	54
2:10	94

INDEX OF BIBLICAL REFERENCES

2:19–20	59	3:10	23
3:26	84	3:23	65
4:5–7	84	4:1	72
5:5	32		
5:22	79	### Colossians	
6:6	122		
6:8	67	1:24	23, 59

Ephesians

1 Thessalonians

1 13	32	1:6	95
6:12–14	112	4:1	72
		4:6	86
		4:17	44, 60, 66

Philippians

1 Timothy

1:23	65		
1:28	53, 95		
3:2–7	119	5:17–18	122

CPSIA information can be obtained
at www.ICGtesting.com
Printed in the USA
LVHW111945160621
690392LV00005B/1067

9 781532 672705